MARY FORD

A to Z of CAKE DECORATING

MARY FORD

A MARY FORD BOOK

Published 1995 by Mary Ford Publications Limited,
Emerson Court, Alderley Road, Wilmslow,
Cheshire SK9 1NX, England.

Typesetting by Russ Design & Production, Salisbury.

ISBN 0 946429 52 9

THE AUTHOR

Mary Ford's warmth and simplicity of teaching style has endeared her to three generations of cake decorators. Her highly popular books have brought her unique step-by-step teaching to a worldwide audience. And yet, Mary is still concerned that each individual reader will come to share her love of cake artistry.

As new techniques emerge, Mary is at the forefront. She enthusiastically practices and develops her craft, and then shares her expertise with her readers, bringing a new and innovative flavour to each book.

Mary is concerned not only with teaching the basics of the craft, but also with building the confidence to tackle more challenging designs and techniques. Her belief is that anyone, by following her method, can become a competent decorator.

Mary Ford acknowledges with grateful thanks the assistance of Mary Smith, Leona Wilkinson and Dawn Pennington in creating some of the items and cakes featured in this book.

CONTENTS

NOTE: WHEN MAKING ANY OF THE RECIPES IN THIS BOOK, FOLLOW ONE SET OF MEASUREMENTS ONLY AS THEY ARE NOT INTERCHANGEABLE.

ALL ABOUT CAKES

Welcome to my new alphabetical guide to cake artistry.

This practical book is a simple step-by-step introduction to the basic skills. It contains completely new material and covers all the latest techniques and decorative items as well as tried and tested classics for royal icing and sugarpaste. As always, everything is laid out in clear, easy to follow stages. I am sure you will have hours of pleasure learning the techniques and applying them to the wide variety of designs in these pages.

The dictionary-style is particularly easy to use. All the recipes, techniques and decorative items are listed in alphabetical order and cross referenced. So, if you want to make a Bas-relief cake, you will find it under B. If you need a spray of flowers you will find it under F. Ribbons loops are, of course, under R, as are Runouts. A Glossary has been included to explain any unfamiliar terms and the index will also help you to locate a particular item.

If you need to know how to prepare a cake for decoration, you will find it under Covering and Coating. If you want to use Almond Paste or Buttercream, you will find them under the appropriate letter of the alphabet. I have also included my tried and tested basic cake recipes. Children tend to prefer a sponge-based cake rather than a rich fruit, but most of the designs are suitable for sponge or fruit cakes.

The different techniques are illustrated by a beautifully decorated cake. The cake designs are extremely versatile. The D.I.Y birthday cake on page 66 would make an excellent retirement cake, for instance, and the Valentine cake on page 192 could easily be adapted to an anniversary or engagement cake.

I have included designs for all levels of decorating experience from the enthusiastic beginner to the most experienced cake artist. If you are just starting out, by following the simple step-by-step guide, you can recreate the easier designs shown. As your skills develop, you can work on more advanced techniques. Once you have gained confidence, then you can move onto combining elements of different

designs, or incorporating new techniques into an old favourite.

All the designs can be varied by using different colours or inscriptions. Some of the cakes can be adapted to a male or female recipient simply by changing the colour. Colours can be chosen to harmonise with a wedding or to match a favourite outfit.

It is always worth practising a design, especially when using a technique for the first time. Any clean, flat surface can be used but an upturned cake tin is particularly useful if you want to assess how the design will look at its actual finished size. It is also worth making extra collars, pieces of lace or flowers in case of breakage, and sufficient coloured sugarpaste or icing should be made as it is virtually impossible to match colours at a later date.

Always allow sufficient time when planning a cake. Fruit cakes ideally need three weeks to mature, almond paste and coatings have to dry before decorating. However, a sponge cake should be made as close to use as possible to ensure freshness. The Madeira cake on page 114 keeps somewhat better than the All-in-one Sponge on page 12 and has a richer flavour. As it has a firmer texture, the Madeira cake can be trimmed easily and is ideal for intricate novelty shapes.

Many of the decorative items can be made in advance and stored in a cardboard box, kept in a dry place. Finished cakes should also be stored, and transported, in cardboard boxes.

I feel sure that you will find all you need to know about cake artistry in the following pages.

Sugar, an essential ingredient in the kitchen, originates in the giant grass-like sugar cane which grows in tropical climates such as the Caribbean, Mauritius and Fiji. It is a flavour enhancer, preservative and natural sweetener as well as contributing to the texture of food.

Sugar can aptly be described as 'a taste of sunshine' because it is manufactured in plants as a direct result of the sun's energy, through a process known as photosynthesis. However, whilst all plants make sugars, commercially produced sugars are extracted only from sugar cane and sugar beet.

The extraction process used by Tate & Lyle removes undesirable impurities and produces the characteristic crystalline structure without the addition of any artificial colourings, flavourings or preservatives.

Nutritionally brown and white sugars are virtually identical, but the distinctive colour and flavour of brown sugar arises from molasses, which is the syrup remaining after all the sugar has been removed from the cane juice. When manufacturing white sugar, the molasses is completely removed whilst the different brown sugars contain more, or less, of the syrup depending on the flavour and colour required.

Therefore, careful selection of the type of sugar used can greatly enhance the finished taste and texture.

Icing Sugar: The finest of all sugars. It dissolves rapidly and is especially used in making icings, smooth toppings, confectionery, meringues and cake frostings. Apart from decorating cakes, icing sugar is perfect for sweetening cold drinks and uncooked desserts, as its fine texture makes it easy to dissolve.

Granulated Sugar: Granulated sugar has a very pure crystal and is an ideal boiling sugar. It can be used for sweetening tea, coffee, sprinkling over cereals or frosting cakes and glasses for decoration.

Caster Sugar: Caster sugar is a free flowing sugar with very fine crystals. Excellent for use in baking cakes and other baked goods as the fine white grains ensure smooth blending and an even texture.

Lyle's Golden Syrup: Golden syrup is a partially inverted syrup produced from intermediate refinery sugar liquors when they are heated in the presence of an acid. It is an ideal sweetener and can be used in cooking and baking to add bulk, texture and taste.

Lyle's Black Treacle: Black treacle is a dark, viscous liquid with a characteristic flavour. It is obtained from cane molasses, a by product of sugar refining.

Demerara Sugar: This sugar has a golden colour with a unique flavour that makes it particularly popular in coffee. The grain is larger than granulated and is ideal for decorating biscuits and cakes, sprinkling over desserts and making crunchy toppings.

Light Brown Soft Sugar: This sugar is fine grained, creamy golden in colour and has a mild syrup flavour. It is best used when creamed with butter or margarine in any recipe that requires a deeper, richer colour and fuller flavour.

Dark Brown Soft Sugar: This sugar is darker with a strong flavour and is ideal for rich fruit cakes, gingerbread, spiced teabreads and puddings.

ALL-IN-ONE FRUIT CAKE

This fruit cake makes the ideal base for any sugarpaste or royal icing celebration cake and has excellent keeping properties. When making a fruit cake, it requires at least three weeks to mature.

For hexagonal, octagonal or petal shaped cakes use recipe for the equivalent round cake. Example, for 20.5cm (8in) heart shape use ingredients for 20.5cm (8in) round cake.

Square tin OR	12.5cm (5in)	15cm (6in)	18cm (7in)	20.5cm (8in)	23cm (9in)	25.5cm (10in)	28cm (11in)
Round tin	15cm (6in)	18cm (7in)	20.5cm (8in)	23cm (9in)	25.5cm (10in)	28cm (11in)	30.5cm (12in)
Sultanas	85g (3oz)	115g (4oz)	170g (6oz)	225g (8oz)	285g (10oz)	340g (12oz)	425g (15oz)
Currants	85g (3oz)	115g (4oz)	170g (6oz)	225g (8oz)	285g (10oz)	340g (12oz)	425g (15oz)
Raisins	85g (3oz)	115g (4oz)	170g (6oz)	225g (8oz)	285g (10oz)	340g (12oz)	425g (15oz)
Candied peel	30g (1oz)	60g (2oz)	60g (2oz)	85g (3oz)	85g (3oz)	115g (4oz)	170g (6oz)
Glacé cherries	30g (1oz)	60g (2oz)	60g (2oz)	85g (3oz)	85g (3oz)	115g (4oz)	170g (6oz)
Lemon rind (lemons)	¼	½	½	1	1½	2	2
Rum/Brandy	½tbsp	½tbsp	1tbsp	1tbsp	1½tbsp	2tbsp	2tbsp
Black treacle	½tbsp	½tbsp	1tbsp	1tbsp	1½tbsp	2tbsp	2tbsp
Soft (tub) margarine	85g (3oz)	115g (4oz)	170g (6oz)	225g (8oz)	285g (10oz)	340g (12oz)	425g (15oz)
Soft light brown sugar	85g (3oz)	115g (4oz)	170g (6oz)	225g (8oz)	285g (10oz)	340g (12oz)	425g (15oz)
Eggs, size 3	1½	2	3	4	5	6	7½
Ground almonds	15g (½oz)	30g (1oz)	45g (1½oz)	60g (2oz)	70g (2½oz)	85g (3oz)	115g (4oz)
Self-raising flour	115g (4oz)	145g (5oz)	200g (7oz)	255g (9oz)	315g (11oz)	400g (14oz)	515g (18oz)
Ground mace	pinch	pinch	pinch	pinch	pinch	pinch	pinch
Mixed spice	¼tsp	½tsp	½tsp	¾tsp	1tsp	1¼tsp	1½tsp
Ground nutmeg	pinch	pinch	¼tsp	¼tsp	½tsp	½tsp	¾tsp
Baking temperature	----150°C (300°F) or Gas Mark 2---			-----------140°C (275°F) or Gas Mark 1-----------			
Approximate baking time	1¾hrs	2hrs	2½hrs	3hrs	3½hrs	4½hrs	6hrs

BAKING TEST Bring the cake forward from the oven at the end of the recommended baking time so that it can be tested. Insert a stainless steel skewer into the centre of the cake and slowly withdraw it. If the cake is sufficiently baked, the skewer will come out as clean as it went in.

Continue baking at the same temperature if the cake mixture clings to the skewer. Test in the same way every ten minutes until the skewer is clean when withdrawn from the cake.

INGREDIENTS

225g sultanas (8oz)	225g soft (tub) margarine (8oz)
225g currants (8oz)	225g soft light brown sugar (8oz)
225g raisins (8oz)	4 eggs, size 3
85g candied peel (3oz)	60g ground almonds (2oz)
85g glacé cherries (3oz)	255g self-raising flour (9oz)
1 lemon	Pinch of ground mace
1tbsp rum/brandy	¾tsp mixed spice
1tbsp black treacle	¼tsp ground nutmeg

EQUIPMENT

20.5cm square cake tin (8in)
OR
23cm round cake tin (9in)
Soft (tub) margarine for greasing
Greaseproof paper
Mixing bowl
Beater
Sieve
Mixing spoon
Skewer

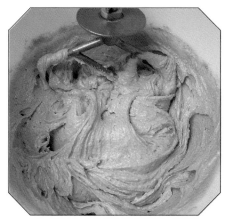 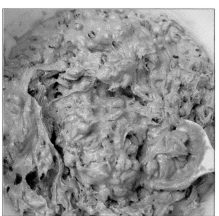 

1 Prepare the tin, fruit and other ingredients as described above. Pre-heat the oven. Place all ingredients, except the fruit, into a mixing bowl. Beat together for 2-3 minutes.

2 Using a spoon, blend in the fruit until well mixed. Place mixture into the tin, level the top and bake.

3 After recommended baking time follow baking test instructions. When baked, leave in the tin until cold. See instructions for storage.

PREPARATION of INGREDIENTS

Weigh all the ingredients separately. Chop cherries in half and carefully clean and remove stalks from all the fruit. Grate the lemon and then mix all the fruit together with rum/brandy. Sift the flour, nutmeg, spice and mace together three times. For better results leave overnight in a warm place 18°C (65°F).

BAKING

Bake in a pre-heated oven at 140°C (275°F) or Gas mark 1 for approximately 2½ to 3hrs.

STORAGE Remove the cake carefully from the tin when it is cold and then take off the greaseproof paper. Wrap the cake in waxed paper and leave in a cupboard for at least three weeks.

PREPARATION of the CAKE TIN

Cut out a length of greasproof paper deeper than the cake tin (enough to cover inside) and then cut along bottom edges at 2.5cm (1in) intervals. Cut a circle or square as required for the base of the tin.
Brush the inside of the tin with soft margarine. Then cover the side with greaseproof paper and place the circle or square into the bottom of the tin. Finally brush the greaseproof paper with margarine.

PORTIONS To estimate the number of portions that can be cut from a finished cake, add up the total weight of all the cake ingredients, almond paste, sugarpaste and/or royal icing. As the average slice of a finished cake weighs approximately 60g (2oz), simply divide the total weight accordingly to calculate the number of portions.

ALL-IN-ONE SPONGE CAKE

This sponge is ideal for birthday cakes and cutting into shapes for novelty cakes.
For hexagonal, octagonal or petal shaped sponges use recipe for the equivalent round sponge. Example, for 20.5cm (8in) heart shape use ingredients for 20.5cm (8in) round sponge.

SPONGE TIN SHAPES   SPONGE TIN SIZES

ROUND	15cm	18cm	20.5cm	23cm	25.5cm	28cm
	(6in)	(7in)	(8in)	(9in)	(10in)	(11in)
SQUARE	12.5cm	15cm	18cm	20.5cm	23cm	25.5cm
	(5in)	(6in)	(7in)	(8in)	(9in)	(10in)
PUDDING BASIN	450ml	600ml	750ml	900ml	1 litre	1.2 Litre
	(¾pt)	(1pt)	(1¼pt)	(1½pt)	(1¾pt)	(2pt)
LOAF TIN		18.5 x 9 x 5cm			21.5 x 11 x 6cm	
		450g (1lb)			900g (2lb)	

Self-raising flour	45g	60g	85g	115g	170g	225g
	(1½oz)	(2oz)	(3oz)	(4oz)	(6oz)	(8oz)
Baking powder	¼tsp	½tsp	¾tsp	1tsp	1½tsp	2tsp
Soft (tub) margarine	45g	60g	85g	115g	170g	225g
	(1½oz)	(2oz)	(3oz)	(4oz)	(6oz)	(8oz)
Caster sugar	45g	60g	85g	115g	170g	225g
	(1½oz)	(2oz)	(3oz)	(4oz)	(6oz)	(8oz)
Eggs	1 size 4	1 size 3	1 size 1	2 size 3	3 size 3	4 size 3

Baking temperature	------------------ 170°C (325°F) or Gas Mark 3 ------------------------------					
Baking time (approximate)	20 min	25 mins	30 mins	32 mins	35 mins	40 mins

PLEASE NOTE: Baking times for sponges baked in pudding basins and loaf tins may take longer.

BAKING TEST When the sponge has reached the recommended baking time, open the oven door slowly and, if the sponge is pale in colour, continue baking until light brown. When light brown, run your fingers across the top gently and the sponge should spring back when touched. If not then continue baking and test every few minutes.

STORAGE When cold the sponge can be deep-frozen for up to six months. Use within three days of baking or defrosting.

PORTIONS A 20.5cm (8in) round sponge should provide approximately sixteen portions when decorated.

For chocolate flavoured sponges:

For every 115g (4oz) of flour used in the recipe add the following ingredients: 2tbsp of cocoa powder dissolved in 2tbsp of hot water, leave to cool then add to the other ingredients in step 3.

For coffee flavoured sponges:

For every 115g (4oz) of flour used in the recipe add 2tsp of instant coffee dissolved in 1tbsp of boiling water, leave to cool then add to the other ingredients in step 3.

For orange or lemon flavoured sponges:

For every 115g (4oz) of flour used in the recipe add the grated rind of one orange or lemon to the other ingredients in step 3.

INGREDIENTS *for Two 20.5cm round sponges (8in) OR Two 18cm square sponges (7in).*

170g self-raising flour (6oz)
1½ tsp baking powder
170g soft (tub) margarine (6oz)
170g caster sugar (6oz)
3 eggs, size 3

BAKING

Bake in a pre-heated oven at 170°C (325°F) or Gas Mark 3 for approximately 30 minutes.

EQUIPMENT

Two 20.5cm round sponge tins (8in)
OR
Two 18cm square sponge tins (7in)
Soft (tub) margarine for greasing
Brush
Greaseproof paper
Mixing bowl
Sieve
Beater
Spatula

1 Grease the tins with soft (tub) margarine, line the bases with greaseproof paper then grease the paper.

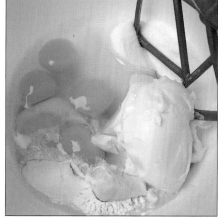

2 Sift the flour and baking powder together twice to ensure a thorough mix. Then place into a mixing bowl with all the other ingredients.

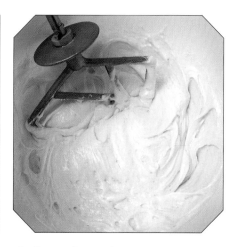

3 Beat mixture for 3-4 minutes until light in colour.

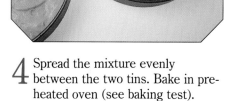

4 Spread the mixture evenly between the two tins. Bake in pre-heated oven (see baking test).

5 When the sponges are baked, leave to cool in the tins for 5 minutes, then carefully turn out onto a wire tray until cold.

6 When cold, sandwich the sponges together with jam and cream then place into a refrigerator for 1 hour before decorating.

ALMOND PASTE

Almond paste is a mixture of uncooked ground almonds, sugar and glucose or eggs. Whereas marzipan is made from cooked ground almonds and sugar. Almond paste can be stored in waxed paper or in a sealed container in a cool, dry place. Do not overmix when making the almond paste. Do not allow the almond paste to come into contact with flour as fermentation may occur.

The almond paste stage in cake decorating is vital in ensuring that smooth layers of icing can be applied later.

Carefully prepare cakes for covering by levelling the top of a domed shape cake or removing the outer edges of a sunken cake. Fill in any imperfections with almond paste and remove any burnt fruit from the surface.

Use icing sugar or caster sugar at all times when rolling out almond paste.

Use boiling apricot purée when fixing almond paste to the cake as this will help prevent mould or fermentation.

When covering a cake, ensure that the layer of almond paste is thick enough to prevent dis-colouring. When covered with almond paste, the cake should have a level top and vertical sides.

After the cake has been covered with almond paste, it should be left to stand in a warm room at about 18°C (65°F) for three to four days. Do not store covered cakes in sealed containers.

See: Covering a cake with almond paste.
To colour almond paste: Blend in food or paste colours. Do not overmix.

USE INGREDIENTS **A** FOR RECIPE WITH EGGS OR INGREDIENTS **B** FOR RECIPE WITHOUT EGGS

INGREDIENTS A

115g caster sugar (4oz)
115g icing sugar (4oz)
225g ground almonds (8oz)
1tsp fresh lemon juice
Few drops of almond essence
1 egg, size 3 or
2 egg yolks, size 3, beaten

INGREDIENTS B

170g icing sugar (6oz)
170g caster sugar (6oz)
340g ground almonds (12oz)
225g glucose syrup, warmed (8oz)

1 **For either recipe:** mix the dry ingredients together and stir to form an even, crumbly texture.

2 Make a well in the centre, then add the remaining ingredients and mix to a firm but pliable paste.

3 Turn out onto a working surface, dusted lightly with caster or icing sugar, and knead until smooth. Store in a sealed container until required.

ALMOND PASTE: EASTER CAKE

INGREDIENTS

20.5cm round cake (8in)
1.25k almond paste (2½lb)
115g royal icing (4oz)
Assorted food colours

EQUIPMENT and DECORATIONS

30.5cm round cake board (12in)
Textured rolling pin
Modelling tool
Fine paint brush
Scissors

Piping tube No.1
Board edge ribbon

*See: Covering a cake
with almond paste Flowers.*

1 Roll out the almond paste then make a basket pattern, using the textured rolling pin. Carefully fix to the cake and board.

2 **To make a daffodil:** Mould almond paste into a cone shape, hollow out then cut into 6 to form petals. Press out and shape each petal with a modelling tool and finger tips. Make and fix the cone-shaped centre.

3 Make a few Polyanthus from almond paste. Roll out and cut leaves and fix all to the cake-top and side as shown. Pipe inscription of choice (No.1). Fix festive decorations as required.

# APPLIQU'E

INGREDIENTS

25.5 x 20.5cm madeira sponge
 (10 x 8in)
1.5k sugarpaste (3lb)
115g royal icing (4oz)
Peach dusting powder
Assorted food colours

EQUIPMENT and DECORATIONS

35.5cm round cake board (14in)
Crimper
Piping tubes No.1 and 2
Small sharp pointed knife

Fine paint brush
Blossom and leaf cutters
Board edge ribbon

1 Cover the board with sugarpaste and crimp around the edge. Trim the corners of the sponge then cover with sugarpaste and fix to the board. Pipe shells (No.2) with royal icing around the base.

2 Using the template as a guide cut out the rabbit and waistcoat from sugarpaste. Leave to dry then brush with dusting powder and decorate as shown. Fix to the cake-top with cooled, boiled water.

3 Cut out sugarpaste blossoms and leaves. Pipe stems (No.2) with royal icing, fix the blossoms and leaves then pipe around the edges (No.1) to form stitches.

4 Cut out and fix small sugarpaste rabbits around the cake-sides. Decorate with small sugarpaste blossoms and piping.

19

INGREDIENTS

25.5cm oval cake (10in)
1.25k almond paste (2½lb)
1.5k sugarpaste (3lb)
115g royal icing (4oz)
Gum tragacanth (optional)
Blue dusting powder
Assorted food colours

EQUIPMENT and DECORATIONS

38cm oval cake board (15in)
Leaf cutter
Flower cutters
Sieve
Fine paint brush
Modelling tools
Piping tube No.1
Board edge ribbon

BAS-RELIEF

Bas-relief produces a two-dimensional sculpted effect. The figure projects less than half its true height, but creates an illusion of height and depth by careful shaping of the contours.

Basic or strengthened sugarpaste (see recipe below) can be used for bas-relief but flower paste is ideal for very intricate work.

The paste, coloured as required, should be rolled to an appropriate thickness and cut with a sharp knife or suitable cutter. The cut edges can be lightly smoothed with a fingertip or a ball-shaped modelling tool. The cut-out should be lightly moistened with cooled, boiled water before assembling.

When working, begin with the areas that will be lower than, or behind, other pieces. Depress or raise as necessary with a ball-shaped modelling tool. If required, a small ball of paste can be used for support.

When painting, care should be taken not to make the paste too wet (test on a dry piece of sugarpaste first). Start with the lighter, delicate areas and then paint-in the darker parts. Finishing touches such as hair or stamens can be piped with royal icing.

Optional: Mix 1 teaspoon of gum tragacanth with 225g (8oz) of sugarpaste for all bas-relief work. Cover and leave for two hours before use.

1 Cover the cake and board with sugarpaste then leave until dry. Brush in the clouds with dusting powder. Make and fix sugarpaste stems. Cut out leaves, mark in the veins and fix.

2 Make the various parts of the flowers, marking the centres with a sieve.

3 Assemble the pieces together then fix to the stems as shown.

4 Mould the mouse and bird and pipe-in the features with royal icing (No.1). Push paste through a wire sieve to create grass effect.

5 Mould the various parts of the hedgehog then fix together using a little moisture. Fold paste around the edge and mark with a pointed modelling tool to form bristles (see step 6).

6 Pipe in the eyes, nose and tongue with royal icing. Fix all the items onto the cake-top. Make and fix sugarpaste flowers and grass around the cake-side. Pipe inscription of choice (No.1).

BAS-RELIEF: BABY

INGREDIENTS

20.5cm round sponge (8in)
2 required
680g sugarpaste (1½lb) for
the covering
225g sugarpaste (8oz) mixed
with 5ml gum tragacanth

(1tsp) optional for the
modelling
115g royal icing (4oz)
Pink dusting powder
Assorted food colours

EQUIPMENT and DECORATIONS

28cm round cake board (11in)
Cocktail stick
Fine paint brush
Piping tube No.1
Board edge ribbon

See: Frills

1 Cover the cake with sugarpaste. Fix to the board then stipple the board with royal icing.

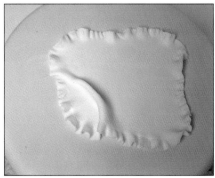

2 Using ordinary sugarpaste or the bas-relief recipe, roll out a small piece, frill the edge with a cocktail stick and fix to the cake-top for the blanket.

3 Make and decorate a sugarpaste pillow. Pipe the shells with royal icing (No.1). Indent the pillow to take the baby's head.

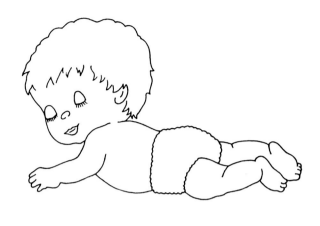

1

Co...
fix
boa...
ren...
out...

4 Mo...
Pai...

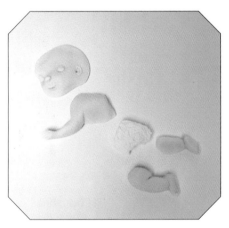

4 Make the various parts of the baby as shown.

5 Fix to the pillow and blanket then pipe the hair with royal icing (No.1). Brush the face with dusting powder and paint in the features.

6 Mould and fix the body, wing and feet of the duck and fix to the cake-side.

7 Mak...
legs...
kne...

7 Make and fix the head, back and bonnet. Paint in the eye.

8 Make and fix a selection of baby ducks as shown. Pipe the flowers (No.1).

9 Make a selection of small animals and fix to the blanket.

INGR

25.5
900g
680g
285g
115g
Asso

1 Cut the sponge to pear shape, then cover the cake and board with sugarpaste. Emboss around the board with an embosser. Pipe shells around the cake-base with royal icing (No.42).

2 Pipe 20 pairs of butterfly wings onto non-stick paper (No.1). Transfer the rose design onto the cake-top and brush embroider the stem and leaves.

3 Brush embroider the outer petals of the rose, using two colours of royal icing.

INGREDIENTS

25.5cm round sponge (10in)
 2 required
1.5k sugarpaste (3lb)
225g royal icing (8oz)
Assorted food colours

EQUIPMENT and DECORATIONS

30.5cm round cake board (12in)
Butterfly embosser
Scriber
Non-stick paper
Piping tubes No.1, 2 and 42
Fine paint brush
Board edge ribbon

See: Brushed embroidery
Lace
Transferring designs

4 Continue adding petals as shown.

5 Complete the rose, then the rosebud.

6 When the wings are dry, pipe a body onto the cake-side (No.2) then insert wings. Repeat around cake. Pipe inscription of choice (No.1).

BIRTHDAY SUNSET

INGREDIENTS

20.5cm square cake (8in)
900g almond paste (2lb)
1.5k royal icing (3lb)
Assorted food colours

EQUIPMENT and DECORATIONS

30.5cm square cake board (12in)
Non-stick paper
Piping tubes No.1 and 2
Fine paint brush

Narrow ribbon
Board edge ribbon

See: Runouts

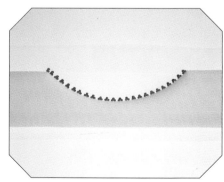

1 Coat the cake and board with royal icing. Outline (No.1) and flood-in the outside section of the runout with royal icing on non-stick paper. Leave to dry for 2 hours.

2 Flood-in the inner section then leave to dry for 6 hours.

3 Pipe the dots as shown (No.1). Leave to dry for 24 hours.

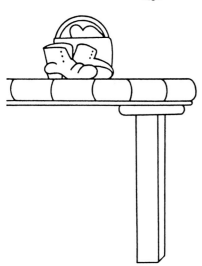

4 Using the template as a guide, pipe-in the sections of the body as shown with royal icing onto non-stick paper. Leave to dry for 5 minutes.

5 Pipe-in the next areas as shown. Leave to dry for 5 minutes.

6 Pipe-in the next areas as shown. Leave to dry for 5 minutes.

7 Pipe-in the next areas as shown. Leave to dry for 5 minutes.

8 Pipe-in the last areas as shown. Leave to dry for 24 hours. Complete the details with fine painted lines.

9 Paint the pier and scenery onto the cake-top.

10 Remove the runout from the paper and fix to the cake-top as shown. Pipe the fishing rod and line (No.1).

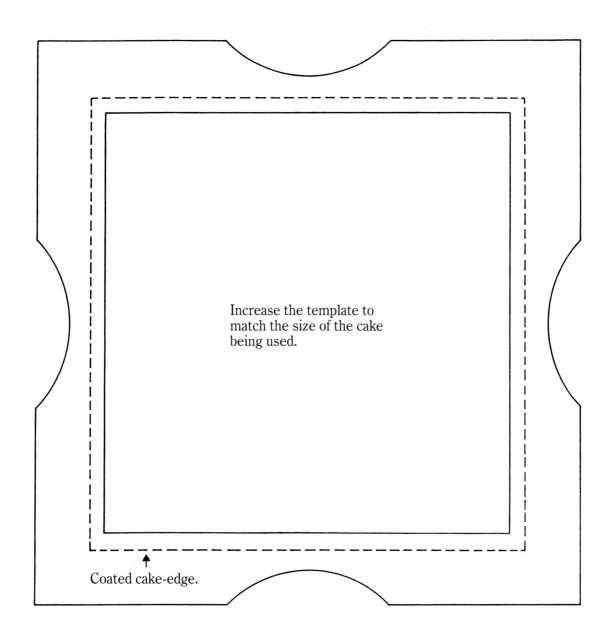

Increase the template to match the size of the cake being used.

↑
Coated cake-edge.

11 Fix the runout collar to the cake-top then pipe shells around the inside edge. (No.2).

12 Fix a narrow ribbon around the cake-side then pipe shells around the cake-base (No.2).

13 Pipe fish shapes onto the cake board (No.1) leave to dry for 10 minutes, then remove with a knife to create the design as shown.

INGREDIENTS

20.5cm square cake (8in)
900g almond paste (2lb)
1.25k sugarpaste (2½lb)
450g royal icing (1lb)
Pink, green and gold dusting powder
Clear alcohol
Assorted food colours

EQUIPMENT and DECORATIONS

28cm square cake board (11in)
Non-stick paper
Piping tubes No.0, 1, 2 and 3
Fine paint brush
Floral spray
Board edge ribbon

See: Filigree Lace

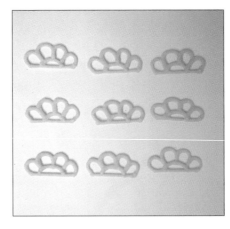

1 Cover the cake and board with sugarpaste. Using the template as a guide, pipe 100 pieces of lace onto non-stick paper with royal icing (No.1).

2 Transfer the floral design onto the cake-top as lightly as possible.

3 Mix dusting powder with a little clear alcohol to form a soft, smooth paste. Brush-in the spray as shown.

4 Pipe the lines and dots shown with royal icing (No.1).

5 Lightly mark two wide bands across the cake-top and down the sides, then pipe filigree as shown (No.0).

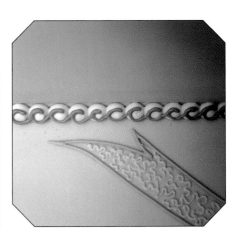

6 Using the template as a guide outline the bow (No.1) then pipe the filigree (No.0).

7 Fix the lace pieces against the band edges at outward angles.

8 Pipe bulbs around the cake-base (No.3). Pipe a scroll on each bulb (No.1). Fix floral decoration of choice.

32

BRODERIE ANGLAISE

INGREDIENTS

18cm round cake (7in)
25.5cm round cake (10in)
2k almond paste (4lb)
2.5k sugarpaste (5lb)
225g royal icing (8oz)
Apricot food colour

EQUIPMENT and DECORATIONS

25.5cm round cake board (10in)
33cm round cake board (13in)
Scriber
Crimper
Frill cutter
Cocktail stick
Piping tube No.1
Narrow ribbon
Board edge ribbon

See: Frilling

To make top ornament: Cut out two rings from modelling paste and one heart shape. Mould two doves. When dry, fix together and decorate with cut-out miniature blossoms.

BRODERIE ANGLAISE

Broderie anglaise is extremely effective when worked in white or very delicate colours. It can be used on sugarpaste collars or worked directly onto the cake. It looks most attractive on wedding or christening cakes.

The basic pattern is pricked into the sugarpaste with a scriber or skewer. The holes can be deepened with the scriber or a knitting needle if required. Using a fine tube, the pattern is then piped to create an open effect.

1 Cover the cakes and board with sugarpaste, then crimp around the board edge and leave until dry. Using a template as a guide divide the cake-side into six and mark with the scriber. Press scriber to form holes shown.

2 Fix narrow ribbon around the cake-base. Cut out, frill and fix sugarpaste following the scribed line around the cake-side.

3 Pipe a line around the edge of each hole with royal icing (No.1). Then pipe floral patterns as required around the cake-side and board.

BRUSHED EMBROIDERY

BRUSHED EMBROIDERY

Brushed embroidery is a delicate technique worked in royal icing using a piping tube and a fine paint brush. It is particularly appropriate for creating foliage and flowers, and is an ideal decoration for any special occasion cake.

The technique can be used on sugarpaste, royal iced or buttercream coated cakes. Freshly made royal icing, to which one teaspoon of piping gel has been added for every four tablespoons of icing, is the easiest medium to work in, as the gel reduces crusting and the icing remains workable for longer.

Icing can be coloured before use, painted with edible food colouring, or dusted with petal dust when completed. If using several different colours of icing, an appropriate number of tubes and bags will be required.

When a suitable design has been selected, it should be transferred to the cake (see Transferring designs). The design is worked from the outside towards the centre, concentrating on a small area at a time.

A fine writing tube (No.1) is used for the outer line, with a finer, inner line if necessary. The icing is then immediately stroked towards the centre with a fine damp (but not wet) brush so that a film of icing covers the design, outlined by a firm edge. The brush should be at a 40° angle and used with a long, smooth stroke to avoid ridges. The icing film will be lighter as it draws towards the centre. The outer line can be overpiped to give more defined edge to petals, etc.

When working on leaves, veins can either be brushed out with a wet paint brush, or piped on with a fine tube.

Highlighting and gentle shading will considerably improve the finished result, especially if attention is given to the natural fall of light, Consistently highlighting one side of a petal or leaf will remove the 'flat' effect. Observing, and reproducing, the natural texture, such as leaf veins, or colouring a deeper shade at the base of a petal, for instance, will ensure the most realistic finish.

Always remember that coloured icing will be almost impossible to remove completely, so extreme care should be taken both with colour and positioning of the icing.

BRUSHED EMBROIDERY: SWAN

INGREDIENTS

25.5cm round cake (10in)
1.25k almond paste (2½lb)
1.5k sugarpaste (3lb)
225g royal icing (8oz)
Piping gel
Assorted food colours

EQUIPMENT and DECORATIONS

33cm round cake board (13in)
Patterned modelling tool
Narrow ribbon
Piping tubes No.1 and 2

Small palette knife
Fine paint brush
Board edge ribbon

See: Transferring designs

For the brushed embroidery piping mixture:
Mix 1 teaspoon piping gel with 4 tablespoons of royal icing. Colour as required.

Prepare the cake as follows:
Cover the cake and board with sugarpaste then immediately press a pattern around the board edge using a modelling tool. Leave until dry then transfer the design to the cake-top and sides.

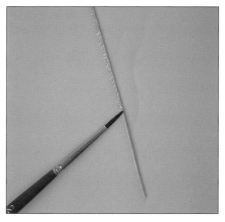

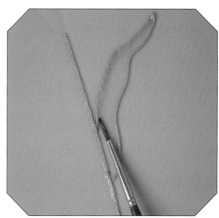

1 Mix the royal icing and piping gel to the recipe and colour a little at a time as required. Pipe the mixture (No.2) for the stem then stroke with a brush as shown.

2 Pipe over the leaf outline (No.2) then gently brush towards the middle to form a fine, thin finish in the centre. Repeat steps 1 and 2 for the bulrush stems and leaves.

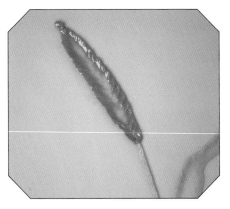

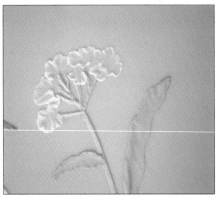

3 Outline the bulrush head (No.2) and brush towards the centre as shown. Complete the remaining heads.

4 Using the same technique create the flower shown (No.1).

5 Using the same technique create the flower shown (No.1).

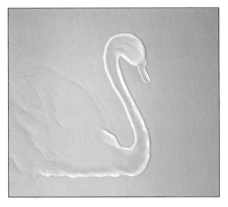

6 Pipe the head, neck and base of the swan and then brush towards the middle as shown (No.1).

7 Pipe the tail and part of the wings (No.1) and brush towards the middle as shown.

8 Finish each wing, working from the outside into the middle, by piping and brushing before the next layer. Complete the swan as shown. Pipe and brush the water shown.

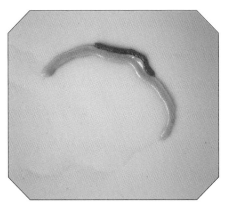

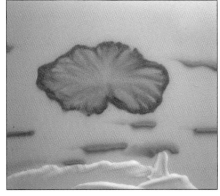

9 Pipe two colours around part of a lily pad (No.1) for the brown and (No.2) for the green, then brush towards the middle.

10 Repeat for each section until completely filled. Repeat steps 9 and 10 for all the lily pads on the cake-top then pipe and brush in the remaining water.

11 Brush embroider the cake-side. Fix the narrow ribbon around the cake-base then pipe the shells with royal icing (No.1).

20.5cm oval cake (8in)
25.5cm oval cake (10in)
2k almond paste (4lb)
2.5k sugarpaste (5lb)
225g royal icing (8oz)
225g flower paste (8oz)
Plum coloured dusting powder
Assorted food colours

25.5cm oval cake board (10in)
30.5cm oval cake board (12in)
 2 required
35.5cm oval cake board (14in)
Piping tube No.1
Fine paint brush
Modelling tools
Edible pen
Floral wire and tape
Calyx cutters

Leaf cutters
Dowelling, 4 required
Cocktail stick
Pointed dowel
Narrow ribbon
Board edge ribbon

*See: Flowers
        Transferring designs*

Preparing the cake and boards:
Using the drawing on page 42 as a guide, fix the boards together in two pairs. Fix sugarpaste around the top rim of the board and trim to shape. Fix the cakes to the boards, then cover the cakes and boards to form the overall shape. Leave until dry.

1 When the sugarpaste on the cake is dry, transfer the design to the cake-sides and rim. Brush embroider the pattern as shown, around the cake-side with royal icing.

2 Fix narrow ribbon around the cake-base. Using the template as a guide, pipe the outline of the pattern onto the cake board with royal icing (No.1).

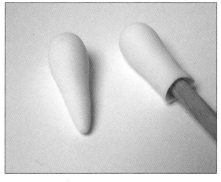

3 **To make a Foxglove:** Mould a long pear shape with flower paste, then hollow out the centre, using a pointed dowel.

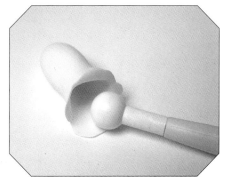

4 With a ball-shaped modelling tool, thin the edge to form the shape shown. Insert hooked floral wire, then make and fix calyx.

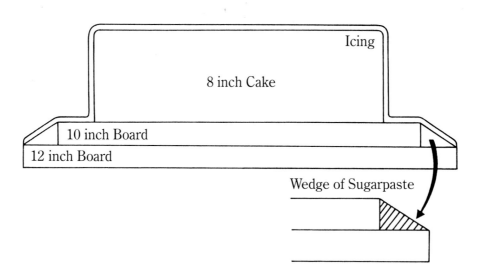

Icing

8 inch Cake

10 inch Board

12 inch Board

Wedge of Sugarpaste

5 Colour the outside of the Foxglove with dusting powder, then mark the inside dots with an edible pen. 20 assorted sizes required for the top ornament and 20 unwired small required for the dowels.

6 Mould long pear shapes onto wire, then make and fix calyx to form buds. Mark larger buds with a groove. 20 assorted sizes required. Cut out a selection of leaf sizes and wire. Cut out an oval base. Leave until dry.

7 When dry, assemble the flowers and leaves, starting from the top and working to the bottom. Then fix to the base, as shown.

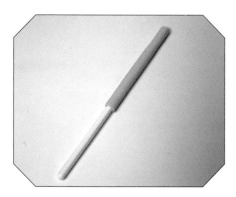

8 Mark bottom tier for position of dowelling. Insert and mark to the depth of the cake. Cut to height required. Cover the dowels with flower paste between the mark and top.

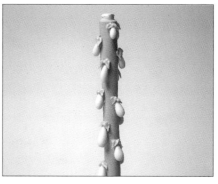

9 Mould miniature buds and fix to the covered dowels. Pipe calyx leaves with royal icing.

10 Fix flowers to the lower sections and pipe further leaves to finish each dowel. Insert into the cake when dry.

BUTTERCREAM

INGREDIENTS

115g butter (4oz) at room
 temperature
170-225g icing sugar, sifted
 (6-8oz)
Few drops vanilla extract
1-2tbsp milk

To obtain best results, always use
fresh butter at a temperature of 18-
21°C (65-70°F).
This recipe can be flavoured and
coloured as desired.

1 Beat the butter until light and fluffy.

2 Beat in the icing sugar, a little at a time, adding the vanilla extract and sufficient milk to give a fairly firm but spreading consistency.

1 **To coat a sponge with butter cream:** Layer sponges together with filling of choice. Spread butter cream onto the cake-top, using a palette knife on a turntable.

2 Spread the butter cream evenly over the cake-top and take the palette knife away, using a sweeping movement to keep the top even.

3 Spread sufficient buttercream around the cake-side using a palette knife.

4 Using a scraper, spread the butter cream evenly around the cake-side.

5 Using a palette knife, gently pull away the buttercream from the cake-top edge as shown.

6 If a patterned side is required use a serrated scraper as shown. Place the coated sponge into a refrigerator to chill before decorating or covering with sugarpaste.

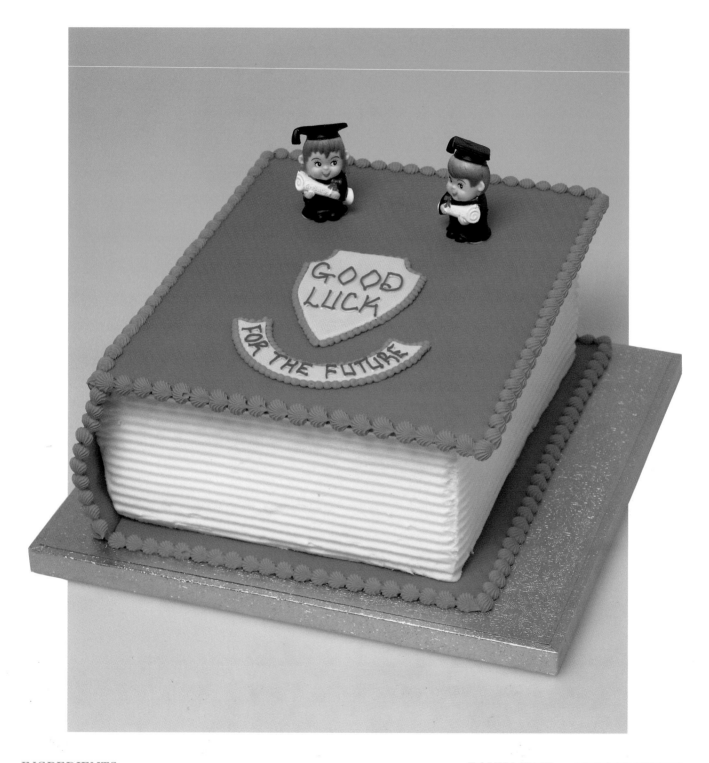

INGREDIENTS

20.5cm square sponge (8in) 2 required
340g buttercream (12oz)
340g sugarpaste (12oz)
115g royal icing (4oz)
Blue, brown and red food colours

EQUIPMENT and DECORATIONS

25.5cm square cake board (10in)
Serrated scraper
Piping tubes No.1, 2 and 43
Decorations of choice

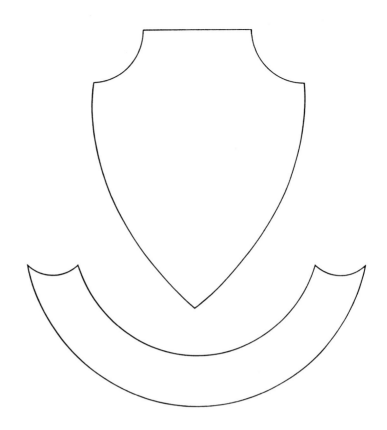

1 Trim the sponges to a book shape. Coat with buttercream, using a serrated scraper for the sides to create page effect. Place in refrigerator to chill.

2 Roll out and cut a piece of sugarpaste for the top cover. Leave until dry. When dry, fix to the cake-top. Cut and fix sugarpaste spine and base cover.

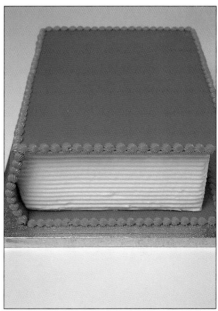

3 Pipe shells along the edges shown with royal icing (No.43).

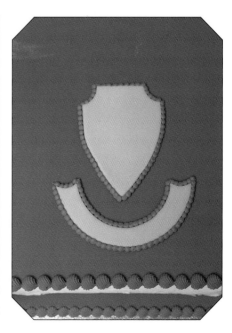

4 Cut out and fix sugarpaste emblem to the cover, then pipe shells around the edge (No.2). Pipe inscription of choice (No.1).

CELESTIAL BIRTHDAY

INGREDIENTS

25.5cm round sponge (10in)
 2 required
900g sugarpaste (2lb)
Assorted food colours
Granulated sugar
Egg white

EQUIPMENT and DECORATIONS

30.5cm round cake board (12in)
Paint brush
Small star cutter
Round cutter
Narrow ribbon
Candles and holders
Board edge ribbon

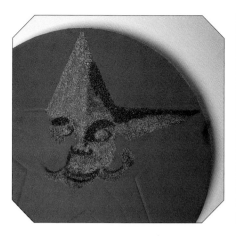

1 Cover the cake and board with sugarpaste. When dry, transfer the template onto cake-top. Brush a small area with egg white, then sprinkle on coloured sugar.

2 Continue moistening small areas and covering with sugar until the picture is complete.

3 Cut out and fix sugarpaste moons and stars onto the cake. Fix ribbon around the cake-base and board edge.

CHILDREN'S CAKE

INGREDIENTS

Sponge baked in a 1.2Lt
 pudding basin (2pt)
900g sugarpaste (2lb)
225g modelling paste (8oz)
115g royal icing (4oz)
Assorted food colours

EQUIPMENT and DECORATIONS

30.5cm round cake board (12in)
Modelling tools
Round cutter
Cocktail stick
Fine paint brush

Piping tubes No.1 and 2
Miniature rose-buds
Flowers and leaves

See: Frills

This is a very versatile cake as it would also be suitable for an adult autumn birthday. It can be adapted for Halloween by adding a cut-out sugarpaste face and appropriate cut-outs to the board.

With a little imagination, the basic technique can also be adapted to create any fairy story, Snow White and the Seven Dwarves for instance, or a favourite nursery rhyme for younger children.

Children like bright colours and easily recognisable characters. You can find your inspiration in books, film or television.

1 Trim the sponge to pumpkin shape, then cover with sugarpaste. With a modelling tool, mark the grooves on the cake-top and down the side.

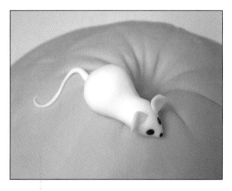

2 Make sugarpaste mice bodies, then make and fix ears and tails. Pipe the eyes with royal icing. (No.1).

3 Make the basic shape for girl with modelling paste. Leave to dry.

4 Place the body into the centre of a round cutter. Roll out a circle of modelling paste and frill the edge with a cocktail stick.

5 Cut a hole in the circle then place over the body and cutter. Gently push in the sides. Cut and frill modelling paste and fix two layers around the base.

6 Cut out and fix a second layer over the dress. Then make and fix a bodice. Decorate with miniature rose buds and piped shells (No.1).

7 Make and fix the head and arms. Decorate with piped hair (No.1). Paint in the facial features. Fix to the board. Make and fix stem. Decorate board with flowers and leaves. Pipe inscription of choice (No.1).

20.5cm round chocolate sponge (8in)
 2 required
225g almond paste (8oz)
Apricot purée
340g plain or milk chocolate covering
 (12oz)
170g white chocolate (6oz)
Pink and green food colouring

25.5cm round cake board (10in)
Pastry brush
Turntable
Palette knife
Non-stick paper
Piping tubes No.2 and 13

Candles and holders
Ribbon bow

*See: Covering a cake with
 almond paste
 Melting chocolate*

1 Layer the sponges together using a filling of your choice. Brush with boiling apricot purée then cover with a thin layer of almond paste. Brush the almond paste with boiling apricot purée.

2 Melt the plain or milk chocolate. With a palette knife and turntable, spread the chocolate evenly over the almond paste. Leave until set.

3 Melt the white chocolate and colour approximately half with green colouring. Using the green chocolate, pipe shells around the sponge base (No.13).

4 Using the remaining white chocolate, colour a small quantity pink. Then, using the templates as a guide, pipe rabbits onto non-stick paper. When set fix to the sponge top. Decorate as required.

CHRISTMAS TIME

INGREDIENTS

20.5cm hexagonal cake (8in)
900g almond paste (2lb)
680g sugarpaste (1½lb)
340g royal icing (12oz)
Assorted dusting powders
Assorted food colours

EQUIPMENT and DECORATIONS

28cm hexagonal cake board (11in)
Granulated sugar
Fine paint brushes
Piping tubes No.3 and 43
Non-stick paper

Narrow ribbon
Board edge ribbon

See: Painting
    Piped figures
    Piped shapes

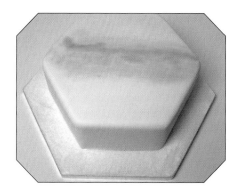

1 Cover the cake with sugarpaste then fix to the board. Stipple royal icing around the remaining board edge and sprinkle with granulated sugar. When dry, brush the cake-top with dusting powders as shown.

2 Using the template as a guide, pipe-in the tree with royal icing. Paint in the background. Leave until dry. Pipe the reindeer onto non-stick paper.

3 Spread royal icing to form the snow covered ground, using a small palette knife, then sprinkle with granulated sugar. Pipe snow onto the tree. Pipe-in small trees. Pipe shells around the cake-base (No.3).

4 When dry, fix the reindeer onto the cake-top then pipe snow around the feet, as shown.

5 Pipe scrolls and shells around the cake-top edge (No.43). Fix ribbons around the cake-side and board edge.

COCOA PAINTING

INGREDIENTS

20.5cm round cake (8in)
680g almond paste (1½lb)
1.25k sugarpaste (2½lb)
225g royal icing (8oz)
Cocoa solution
Pink and ivory food colours

EQUIPMENT and DECORATIONS

28cm round cake board (11in)   Non-stick paper
Paint brushes   Ribbon bow
Cocktail stick   Board edge ribbon
Scalloped cutter
Piping tubes No.0, 1 and 4   *See: Frills*
                                         Lace

COCOA PAINTING

Cocoa painting is a most attractive medium. Inspiration from designs can be found in sepia or black and white pictures, in the slate plaques on which animals are often featured, or in cards which have been printed in several shades of one colour. Proficient artists will enjoy creating their own design.

Painting can either be directly onto the cake or onto a sugarpaste or almond paste plaque, which could be removed and kept as a memento of the occasion.

The sugarpaste plaque can be lightly coloured before rolling out. The background colour depends on the subject chosen and the colour of the cake.

The design should be sketched or traced with minimal detail onto the cake or plaque. If too many lines are used, they may well show through and affect the finished appearance.

Begin by painting the background areas in the lightest shade and then progress to the medium tone, and then to the darker shade. Finally fill in the eyes, etc, and any shadows with the very dark mix. Once the plaque is dry, a scalpel can be used to scratch or scrape away some of the colour to form highlights and textures such as fur or grass.

COCOA SOLUTION

To prepare the cocoa, place a teaspoon of white vegetable fat, coconut oil or cocoa butter (available from health stores) into each of four small heat proof containers. Place the containers in a pan of boiling water. Add a little cocoa to the first container to produce a very light shade. Gradually add more cocoa to the other containers to produce darker shades. The last container should be a dark brown shade for filling in features and shadows. The water may need to be reheated from time to time while painting if the solution becomes too stiff. The containers can be covered with a cloth and left overnight if necessary, simply reheating the water the next day.

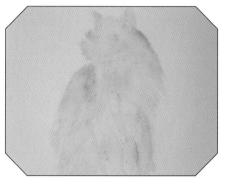

1 Cover the cake and board with sugarpaste. Pipe 80 pieces of lace onto non-stick paper with royal icing (No.1). Leave until dry. Make the cocoa solutions. Transfer the design onto the cake-top and paint the first layer.

2 Using the next, darker shade, brush the area shown.

3 Brush on the final darkest shade to complete the picture.

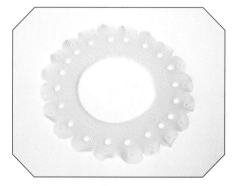

4 Roll out and cut sugarpaste frill. Using a No.4 piping tube cut out a hole in each curve. Cut the circle and fix onto the cake-top. Make and fix sufficient to complete the top and base.

5 Pipe a line around each hole with royal icing (No.0) then pipe rope (No.1) around the edges of the top frill. Pipe shells around the inside edge and then fix the piped lace pieces.

6 Repeat step 5 around the cake-base. Fix ribbon around the cake-side and a bow to the cake-top.

COVERING and COATING

COVERING A CAKE WITH ALMOND PASTE

These steps are for covering cakes with almond paste ready for coating with royal icing.

1 **For a round cake:** Roll out almond paste using icing or caster sugar for dusting. Brush top of cake with boiling apricot purée. Upturn cake onto the almond paste and then cut around as shown.

2 Place cake on board. Roll out almond paste into strip that is long and wide enough to cover side of cake in one piece. Spread a thin layer of apricot purée over paste.

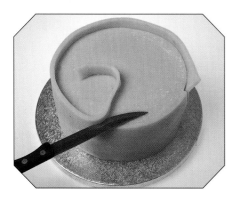

3 Fix the almond paste to the side of the cake and trim off the surplus with a sharp knife. Leave to dry for 3 days before coating with royal icing.

4 **For a square cake:** Roll out paste into half the thickness used on the cake top. Cut into 4 equal strips to fit the sides of a square cake. Spread apricot purée on the strips.

5 Fix strips to the sides of the cake. Trim away any surplus cutting towards the centre using a sharp knife. Leave for 3 days before coating with royal icing.

COATING CAKES WITH ROYAL ICING

Royal icing should be made at least 24 hours before use as this allows the strength of the albumen to develop, producing a smooth consistent texture that is ideal for spreading. The icing should be coated onto an almond paste covered cake that has been allowed to dry completely.

CAKE BOARDS: Use strong, thick boards to prevent damage when moving. Ensure that it is positioned exactly on the board before commencing.

COLOURED ROYAL ICING: Pale coloured royal icing: First coat white. Second a pale shade of the final colour. Last coat actual colour.
For strong coloured royal icing: First coat half strength. Second three quarter strength. Final coat full strength.
Colour enough icing for coating tiers and any other requirements you may have as it will be virtually impossible to match later.
Do not add any blue to lemon icing as this will discolour icing.

COATING CAKES: Use at least three layers of royal icing. Make the first the thicker (to remove any uneveness in almond paste); second layer should be half thickness of first; final layer creates smooth finish. Allow to dry between layers.
Do not dip palette knife or ruler into water when applying the icing.
Carefully trim each layer when dry, using a sharp knife.
Coloured icing tends to dry patchily if coatings have been applied unevenly.

DRYING: Drying can take twice as long under adverse weather conditions. An airing cupboard is ideal for drying cakes. Avoid drying in a humid kitchen or under direct sunlight.
Coating must be perfectly dry and stable before tiering (one week before required). Recorddates for ease of reference.

STORING: Store in a cardboard box to allow cake to breathe and air to circulate to keep it dry.

TIERING: See Wedding Cakes.

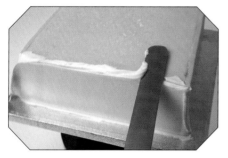

1 Coating straight sided cakes: Coat opposite sides of the cake with royal icing and then remove any surplus. Leave to dry for 12 hours. Repeat the procedure for the other 2 sides.

2 With a palette knife spread royal icing evenly over top of cake using a paddling motion. Level icing using a ruler until top of cake is smooth. Then remove surplus from edges and leave to dry for 12 hours. Repeat steps 1 and 2 for a further 2 layers.

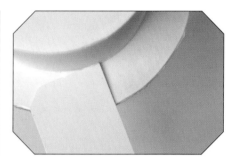

3 Coating the cake board: Spread royal icing over the cake board using a palette knife. Then smooth the icing by holding a scraper and revolving the turntable. Clean the sides and leave for 12 hours.

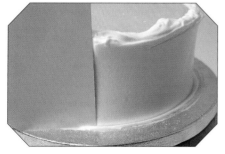

4 Coating a round cake: Carefully position the cake on turntable. Spread royal icing around the cake-side using a palette knife. Smooth the icing using a scraper against the cake-side and revolving the turntable one complete turn. Repeat the process until smooth.

5 Using a palette knife, remove any surplus icing from the cake-top and cake board. Then leave to dry for 12 hours.

6 Spread icing evenly over cake-top using a palette knife. Level the icing with a steel ruler. Remove surplus icing from the edge of cake and leave to dry for 12 hours. Repeat all the steps for 2 more layers.

COVERING and COATING

COVERING CAKES WITH SUGARPASTE

1 **To cover a round or square sponge:** Coat the cake-side and top with a thin layer of buttercream. Chill for 1 hour in the refrigerator.

2 When chilled, roll out the sugarpaste and place over the cake, using the rolling pin.

3 Smooth the paste over the top, then down the side, using palm of hand. Trim around the cake-base or board edge. Leave until dry before decorating.

1 **Covering a round or square fruit cake:** Fill-in any imperfections with almond paste. Brush boiling apricot purée over the cake-top and sides.

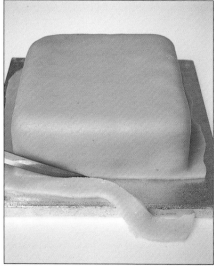

2 Roll out almond paste, dusting with icing and place over the cake, using the rolling pin. Then press firmly to the cake-top and sides using palm of hand to expel any trapped air. Leave to dry for 24 hours.

3 Brush the almond paste with cooled boiled water. Roll out sugarpaste, dusting with icing sugar and place over the cake. Smooth to expel any trapped air. Trim paste and leave until dry before decorating.

CRIMPING

Crimping is an easy way to create patterns in sugarpaste or almond paste. It should be carried out immediately after covering before the paste has dried. Plaques or board edges can also be crimped.

Place a rubber band around the crimping tool to bring the teeth 6mm (¼in) apart. Dip the teeth into sieved icing sugar and tap off the surplus. Push the teeth into the paste, squeeze together then gently release and raise the crimper. Repeat evenly around the cake. To achieve the best results, use the same pressure on each crimp.

It is well worth practising crimping on a spare piece of paste until spacing and depth of crimp are even.

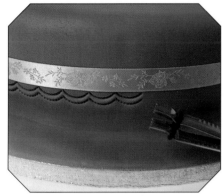

1 Cover the cake with sugarpaste, then pin ribbon around the middle of the cake-side. Immediately crimp the sugarpaste below the ribbon.

2 Crimp just above the ribbon, keeping a regular pattern. Then carefully remove the ribbon.

3 Using the heart shaped crimpers, close together and press into the cake-top to create flowers.

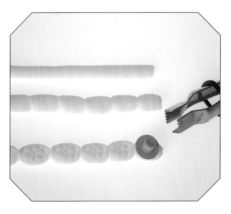

4 Mould sugarpaste into a long roll, squeeze together with crimpers, then press a floral embosser onto each section.

INGREDIENTS

20.5cm round cake (8in)
680g almond paste (1½lb)
900g sugarpaste (2lb)
115g royal icing (4oz)
Violet and yellow food colours

EQUIPMENT and DECORATIONS

28cm round cake board (11in)
Ribbon
Crimpers
Embossers
Miniature blossom cutter
Piping tube No.1
Board edge ribbon

5 Fix the roll around the cake-base then leave until dry.

6 Cut out and fix miniature blossoms around the middle of the cake-side, then pipe stems, leaves and centres with royal icing (No.1).

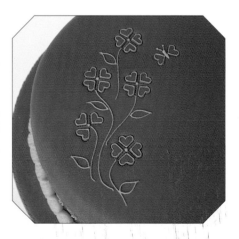

7 Pipe a line over each petal, then pipe stems and leaves as shown. Pipe inscription of choice and fix ribbon around the board.

EQUIPMENT and DECORATIONS

INGREDIENTS

25.5cm square cake (10in)
1.5k almond paste (3lb)
1.5k royal icing (3lb)
Cream and Burgundy colouring

28cm square cake board (11in)
Piping tubes No.1, 2 and 3
Non-stick paper
Ribbon bows
Floral spray

Horseshoes and motto
Board edge ribbon

See: Filigree
  Piped shapes

DO-IT-YOURSELF

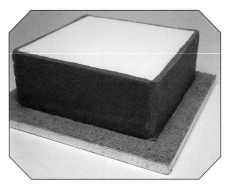

1 Cover the cake with almond paste and fix to the board. Cover the top with sugarpaste, then cover the sides. Spread royal icing around the board then sprinkle with demerara sugar.

2 Using a rule as a guide mark the cake-sides to form brick effect, then pipe the lines shown with royal icing (No.3) for the mortar.

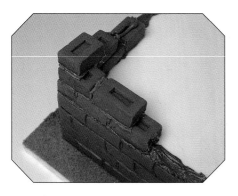

3 Make and fix sugarpaste bricks to one corner and pipe in the mortar.

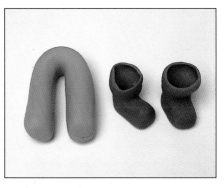

4 Mould sugarpaste into first stage of the trousers and a pair of boots.

5 Press the top of the trousers with thumbs to form the shape shown, then fix into the boots. Make and fix a belt and loops.

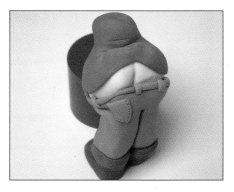

6 Mould and fix bottom and shirt. Support in a leaning position.

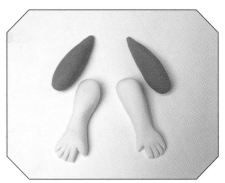

7 Mould the first stage of the arms and shirt sleeves as shown.

8 Pinch out the sleeves, fix onto the arms then fix to the body. Place onto the built up bricks.

9 Mould and fix the head, paint on the hair, then make and fix hat and trowel. Decorate with appropriate items, then pipe inscription (No.1).

20.5cm square cake (8in)
900g almond paste (2lb)
1.5k sugarpaste (3lb)
225g royal icing (8oz)
Demerara sugar
Assorted food colours

28cm square cake board (11in)
Rule
Modelling tools
Fine paint brush

Piping tubes No.1 and 3
Board edge ribbon

See: Modelling

EASTER

INGREDIENTS

20.5cm round madeira cake (8in)
680g sugarpaste (1½lb)
225g royal icing (8oz)
Assorted food colours

EQUIPMENT and DECORATIONS

28cm round cake board (11in)
Non-stick paper
Fine paint brush
Piping tubes No.0, 1 and 2

Board edge ribbon

See: Extension work
Figure piping
Lace

1 Cut a thin layer off the cake-top, cut out a 13cm (5in) circle. Fix the ring to the cake-top and then cover with sugarpaste. When dry, paint the background with food colours using the template as a guide.

2 Trace the figure templates onto paper and cover with non-stick paper. Using royal icing without glycerin, fill-in the parts shown. Leave to dry for 10 minutes.

3 Fill-in the further parts as shown. Leave to dry for 10 minutes.

68

4 Fill in the further parts as shown. Leave to dry for 10 minutes.

5 Fill-in the further parts as shown. Leave to dry for 10 minutes.

6 Fill-in the final parts as shown. Leave to dry for 24 hours then decorate as shown. Pipe 120 pieces of lace (No.0). Leave until dry.

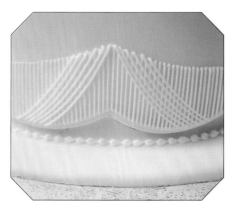

7 Pipe shells around the cake-base (No.1). Pipe curved lines around the cake-side (No.2) twice, then (No.1) three times. Pipe the suspended lines as shown.

8 Fix the figures to the cake-top. Then fix the lace around the cake-top and side.

9 Pipe rabbit shapes around the cake-side (No.1) and then paint the ground as shown. Pipe inscription of choice (No.1).

EMBOSSING

Embossing is a very quick and easy way to decorate a cake.

Practically any raised, patterned surface can be used for embossing so there is plenty of scope for improvisation. Buttons, badges, decorative cutlery, bottle tops and the end of a paintbrush can all be utilised. However, purpose-made embossers such as the one used here can be purchased from specialist shops.

Embossing must be carried out on almond paste or sugarpaste before it dries, using an even pressure. It can be coloured with dusting powder or edible food colour and larger areas such as flowers can be filled with piping gel.

INGREDIENTS

20.5cm square cake (8in)
900g almond paste (2lb)
900g sugarpaste (2lb)
115g royal icing (4oz)
Assorted food colours

EQUIPMENT and DECORATIONS

28cm square cake board (11in)
Modelling tool
Embossers
Fine paint brush
Piping tube No.1
Board edge ribbon

1 Cover the cake and board with sugarpaste. Immediately press a floral embosser onto the cake-top to form the impressions shown.

2 Press the embosser into the cake-side, then use a butterfly design embosser. Press the fan shaped modelling tool around the cake board edge as shown. Leave to dry.

3 When dry, colour the flowers using a fine paint brush.

4 Join the flowers together with painted stems and leaves.

5 Paint the butterflies and fan shapes. Pipe inscription of choice with royal icing (No.1).

EMBROIDERY

INGREDIENTS

20.5cm petal shaped cake (8in)
680g almond paste (1½lb)
900g sugarpaste (2lb)
170g royal icing (6oz)
Assorted food colours

EQUIPMENT and DECORATIONS

25.5cm petal shaped cake board (10in)
Crimper
Piping tube No.1
Board edge ribbon

Embroidery has been used as a decoration for centuries and inspiration can be found in old samplers, embroidered tableclothes or craft books. The stitches fall into two basic types: straight stitches used for formal patterns on royal iced cakes, and softer, rounded stitches which look well on the more flowing lines of sugarpaste cakes.

Before commencing piping, all the colours of icing should be mixed and placed in small piping bags with a No.0 or 00 tube. A few teaspoons of icing in each colour will be more than sufficient.

When piping, work the background first and then the main areas. Complete each section of the design at a time, changing colours as required. A damp paint brush can be smoothed over joins if necessary.

It is easier to work from left to right, unless you are left handed, and care should be taken that all stitches which cross over another line do so in the same direction. A slight variation in pressure may be needed for areas that need emphasis.

If embroidery is used for tiered cakes, the designs should be carefully scaled down for each tier – a photocopier will enlarge or reduce designs very quickly.

71

INGREDIENTS

20.5cm square cake (8in)
900g almond paste (2lb)
680g sugarpaste (1½lb)
115g flower paste (4oz)
115g royal icing (4oz)
Green and peach dusting powder
Green, peach and yellow food colours

EQUIPMENT and DECORATIONS

28cm square cake board (11in)
Crimper
Flower cutter
Miniature pear shaped cutter
Fine paint brush
Piping tube No.1
Narrow ribbon
Ribbon bows
Board edge ribbon

1 Cover the cake with sugarpaste and fix to the board. Then cover the board with sugarpaste. Cut out floral shapes from flower paste. Cut out pear shapes and trim to triple petals. 30 pieces required.

2 Transfer the design onto the cake-top and cake-sides. Brush-in the leaves and flowers with dusting powder as shown.

3 Pipe short lines over the stems, leaves and flowers with royal icing (No.1) to represent stitch embroidery.

4 Repeat the dusting and piping onto the cake-side design, then fix narrow ribbon around the cake-base.

5 Fix the cut-outs to the front edges of the narrow ribbon and then to the back cake-top edges. Pipe and decorate inscription of choice (No.1). Fix ribbon bows and ribbon round the cake board edge.

ENGAGEMENT

INGREDIENTS

20.5cm round cake (8in)
680g almond paste (1½lb)
900g royal icing (2lb)
115g sugarpaste (4oz)
Assorted dusting powders
Assorted food colours

EQUIPMENT and DECORATIONS

28cm round cake board (11in)
Non-stick paper
Piping tubes No.1, 2 and 3
Blossom cutters
Fine paint brush
Board edge ribbon

See: Painting

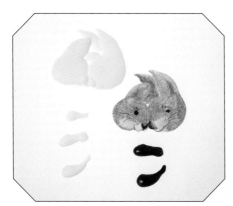

1 Using the template as a guide, pipe-in the heads and three shoes onto non-stick paper with royal icing without glycerin. When dry, paint the heads and two shoes as shown.

2 Make the two bodies with sugarpaste and leave to dry.

3 Trace the lamp and railings onto the cake-top then brush with liquid colours and dusting powder.

4 When dry carefully fix the rabbits to the picture.

5 Pipe shells around the cake-base (No.2). Pipe curved lines around the cake-side (No.1). Cut out and fix sugarpaste flowers, pipe the leaves and bows as shown.

6 Pipe shells around the cake-top (No.3). Pipe a line over the shells (No.1). Pipe filigree around the cake board edge (No.1).

EQUIPMENT

When purchasing equipment, it is always worth buying the best quality as this will not rust, bend or chip and may last a lifetime with careful use. However, much of the equipment required can be improvised from items already in the kitchen. Where possible, wooden spoons and plastic bowls should be set aside for icing only as they can absorb strong flavours and taint the icing. Metal bowls, other than stainless steel, are not suitable. Glass or earthenware bowls are ideal provided they have no cracks. Where possible, use food approved spoons and plastic bowls. A mixer is extremely useful for making coverings and coatings.

Most supermarkets now sell a good range of ready to use coatings and coverings, cake decorating items and colours.

Ball shaped modelling tool

A ball shaped modelling tool can be purchased from specialist suppliers. It makes modelling much easier.

Cake boards and stands

Always use a thick cake board which will support the weight of the cake. Boards are available in many different sizes and an appropriate size and shape for the design should be selected. Thin cake cards are available for placing between decorative items and the cake, or between the cake and a paper or fabric covered board.

Stands for a special occasion can be hired from specialist shops. Unusual shaped boards may also be available but boards can be cut from wood and then covered.

Covering a board creates a unique look for a cake and the covering can be fabric or paper. Many of the foil papers now available are ideal for producing a subtle sheen. Paper covering should be stuck to the board with laundry starch or cornflour, whilst fabric can be stuck to the back of the board with fabric adhesive. Fabric can also be gathered with running stitches and pulled up to enclose the whole board. When making boards for tiered cakes, remember to stick an extra circle to the back of the board. Non food approved fabric or paper must have a cake card between it and the cake. Ribbon can be used to cover the edge of the board.

Boards may also be covered with two coats of royal icing around the ready-positioned cake, or the cake and board can be covered in sugarpaste.

Colours

Confectioner's dusting powder, edible paste or liquid colours and food-approved pens are available from specialist suppliers or supermarkets.

Crimpers

Crimpers are available in a wide variety of material and designs. A good crimper will spring back into place but it is not so powerful that it needs hard pressure to close.

Cutters

Purpose made cutters can be purchased from specialist suppliers but can be improvised from cardboard templates if necessary.

Embossers

Purpose made embossers are raised cutters impressions which are available from most specialist shops. They can be improvised from buttons etc.

Leaf shaped piping bag

Instructions for making a leaf shaped piping bag are given on page 140.

Palette knives

Stainless steel palette knives with a firm blade are required for mixing in colour and for coating cakes. An 18cm (7") and a 10cm (4") knife should be sufficient. A 38cm (15") straight edge is needed for smoothing royal icing or buttercream. This can be stainless steel or rigid plastic.

Paint brushes

A small paint brush with a fine point is useful for colouring flowers and painting in features.

Piping bag

Instructions for making a piping bag are shown on page 134.

Piping gel

Piping gel can be purchased from specialist suppliers or supermarkets. For recipe see page 145.

Rolling pins

A good quality, heavy and smooth rolling pin is essential for rolling out pastes. Smaller, plastic rolling pins will also be useful. Textured rolling pins are also available. Nylon spacers achieve an even thickness of paste.

Rulers

Stainless steel rulers are useful for coating cakes and indenting pastes, etc.

Scriber

A scriber is useful for transferring patterns to cakes but can be improvised using the end of a skewer or sharp, pointed knife.

Tools for coating

A stiff, stainless steel palette knife is ideal for spreading royal icing, and a stainless steel ruler can be used for flattening and levelling the top surface. Side scrapers which are not too flexible should be selected as this will produce a smooth finish. Plastic or stainless steel scrapers are best. When using a side scraper, the fingers should be spread across the width of the scraper to ensure even pressure when rotating the turntable. A turntable makes the work much easier. It should be capable of supporting a heavy cake with a minimum diameter of 23cm (9in) to enable safe carriage of a loaded 51cm (20in) cake board. A non-slip base is essential, and the turntable should turn freely. A turntable for small cakes can be improvised by using an upturned cake tin or plate if necessary.

Veiners

Purpose made veiners can be purchased from specialist outlets or can be improvised using a cocktail stick.

Wires and tapes

These are available from most specialist outlets.

EXTENSION WORK

Extension work is also known as curtain borders. It makes a striking decoration for wedding and anniversary cakes on royal iced or sugarpaste cakes.

The technique is worked in freshly made royal icing, with a fine tube. It offers scope for improvisation and variation. The bottom edge of the border is usually scalloped but the top edge can be straight, curved, scalloped or pointed and can incorporate lace or an

appropriate motif for the occasion such as hearts or bells.

To ensure even working of scallops, work from a pattern. Cut a strip of greaseproof paper the exact length of one side of a square cake or the circumference of a round cake, and the height of the border. Then fold the strip until the desired width of scallop is achieved. Cut the bottom into a shallow curve. The top should be trimmed into the required shape or left straight as desired.

INGREDIENTS

20.5cm square cake (8in)
900g almond paste (2lb)
900g sugarpaste (2lb)
225g royal icing (8oz)
115g flower paste (4oz) optional
Blue food colour

EQUIPMENT and DECORATIONS

25.5cm square cake board (10in)
Non-stick paper
Glass headed pins
Piping tubes No.0 and 1
Curved mould
Round cutter
Fine paint brush

Ribbon bows
Horseshoes
Blossoms
50 pieces of piped lace

See: Lace

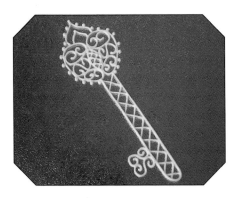

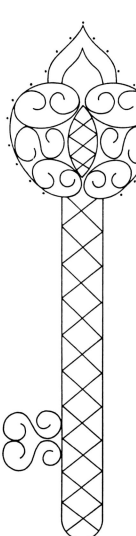

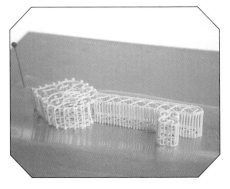

1 **To make a key:** Using the template as a guide, pipe the lines and dots shown with royal icing (No.1) without glycerin onto non-stick paper. Leave until dry. 2 required.

2 When dry, place a small piece of polystyrene onto each end of one key, then remove the other key from the paper and place on top of the polystyrene.

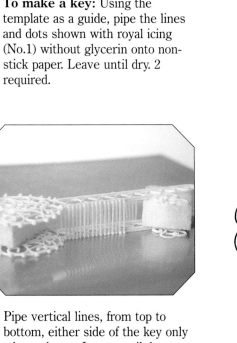

3 Pipe vertical lines, from top to bottom, either side of the key only where shown. Leave until dry.

4 When dry, carefully remove the two pieces of polystyrene and pipe the remaining lines around the keys. Leave until dry then remove from the paper.

BRIDGE AND EXTENSION WORK

First method: Basic bridge and extension work.

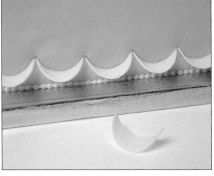

1 Cut semi-circles of flower paste and place into a curved mould until dry for the bridge. Make more than required to surround the cake-sides.

2 When the semi-circles are dry, cover the cake with sugarpaste. Scratch a line around the cake-side as a guide for fixing the bridge sections and another for the level of the piped lines.

3 Pipe shells around the cake-base (No.1). Push the bridge pieces into the cake-side. Then pipe the lines shown using royal icing without glycerin (No.1).

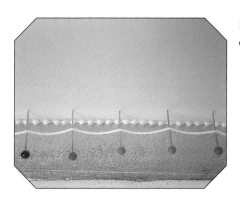

1 Cover the cake with sugarpaste. When dry, pipe shells around the cake-base with royal icing (No.1). Lightly scratch a line around the cake-sides for the level of the pins and for the level of the piped lines.

Second method: Floating bridge and extension work.

Push lightly greased glass headed pins equal distances apart into the cake-sides. Pipe a line using royal icing without glycerin over the pins as shown (No.1).

2 When the line is dry, pipe lines from the cake-side to the suspended lines. Remove the pins when the lines are dry.

Third method: Standard bridge and floating work.

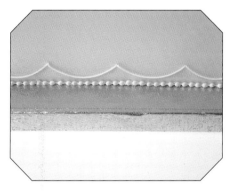

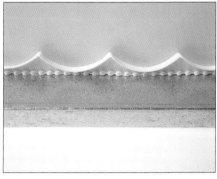

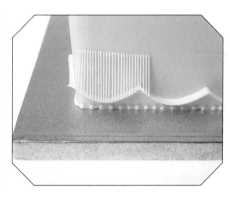

1 Cover the cake with sugarpaste. When dry, scratch two faint guide lines around the cake-sides, top line for extension piped lines and bottom for curved bridge.
Divide the bottom line into equal spaces. Pipe shells around the cake-base (No.1) then the curved lines as shown.

2 Pipe as many times as necessary against against the curved line to build out the width required. Leave to dry to avoid the bridge collapsing.

3 When the bridge lines are dry, pipe a few extension lines from the scratch line to bridge. Clean off the ends with a fine paint brush, then repeat the process until the cake-sides are complete.

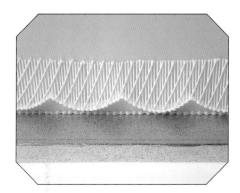

4 When the lines are dry, pipe diagonal lines to form the pattern shown.

5 Carefully fix the lace pieces along the top edge, at the angle shown.

6 Fix the key to the cake-top, pipe inscription of choice (No.1) and decorate with ribbon bows and horseshoes.

Filigree is a delicate fill-in technique which should be worked in freshly-made royal icing with a fine tube. It can be worked directly onto the cake or onto non-stick paper for a three dimensional shape which is assembled when dry.

When working, keep the tube on the cake surface, and pipe continuous, random shaped lines.

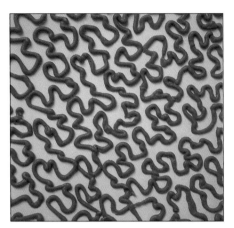

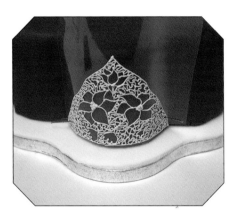

1 Cover the cakes with sugarpaste. Cover the boards with sugarpaste and remove the area to be covered by the cake. Then fix the cakes to the boards. Draw the template onto paper seven times and fix three to the side of each tin in which the cakes were baked. Place the tins on their sides. Tape non-stick paper over each template. Pipe the outline of the template and then the outline of the flowers with royal icing (No.1). Pipe filigree between the spaces as shown (No.1). Leave until dry. Then repeat again for the remaining three sections. Meanwhile pipe one whole section and two half sections onto a flat surface and leave until dry. When dry, fix the side sections to the cake board as shown.

2 Pipe shells around the base of each section (No.1). Cut out and fix sugarpaste blossoms between the sections as shown.

3 Fix the top sections together and leave for 1 hour. Pipe shells around the base and dots onto the edges (No.1). Decorate the cake with sugarpaste blossoms and sugar doves.

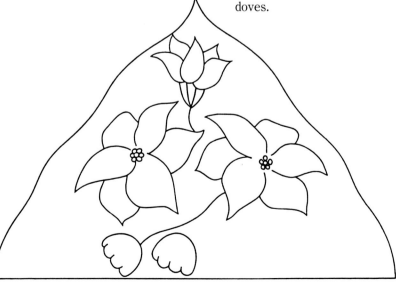

15cm round cake (6in)
20.5cm petal shaped cake (8in)
1.5k almond paste (3lb)
1.5k sugarpaste (3lb)
450g royal icing (1lb)
Burgundy and cream food colouring

25.5cm round cake board (8in)
28cm petal shaped cake board (11in)
Non-stick paper
Piping tube No.1
Blossom cutter
Sugar doves
Board edge ribbon

INGREDIENTS

Small bell shaped cake
15cm round cake (6in)
25.5cm petal shaped cake (10in)
2.5k almond paste (5lb)
4k sugarpaste (8lb)
450g royal icing (1lb)
Yellow, green and orange food
 colours

EQUIPMENT and DECORATIONS

15cm round cake board (6in)
23cm round cake board (9in)
35.5cm petal-shaped cake board
 (14in)
Fine paint brush
Crimper
Non-stick paper
Piping tubes No.1 and 2
Narrow ribbons
Board edge ribbon

See: Extension work
 Ribbon loops

PREPARATION

Cover the cakes and boards with
sugarpaste and then immediately
crimp around the board edge.
Leave until dry. Using the template
as a guide pipe 120 pieces of lace
onto non-stick paper with royal
icing (No.1). Leave until dry.

1 Transfer the designs onto the cake-
side and then paint-in the colours.
Pipe shells around the cake-base
(No.2).

2 Tilt the cake, then pipe a series of
lines against the guide line to the
width required (No.2) between 3
and 6 lines can be used. When dry,
brush over the lines with softened
royal icing to form the bridge.

3 Pipe suspended lines from the top
guide line to the bridge as shown
(No.1).

4 When the lines are dry, pipe dots onto each line in an irregular pattern (No.1).

5 Pipe shells along the top edge and against the edge of the bridge (No.1).

6 Fix the lace in even circles onto the cakes as shown. Fix ribbon around the board edges. Decorate top tier with ribbon bows and loops, then fix lace pieces around the cake board.

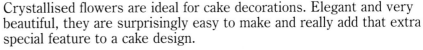

FLOWERS: CRYSTALLISED

Crystallised flowers are ideal for cake decorations. Elegant and very beautiful, they are surprisingly easy to make and really add that extra special feature to a cake design.

Before starting check that the flowers you intend to crystallise are edible and have not been sprayed with pesticide.

There are many edible flowers and leaves to choose from and you will probably find a selection in the garden (see list below). Flowers from any bulb such as daffodils, snowdrops or lily-of-the-valley should never be used.

Carefully select the flowers you intend to crystallise and pick when they have just opened and are completely dry (usually around midday). Make sure that they are free from insects and discard any that are not perfect.

The flowers crystallised by the method shown here should be used within a few days. However, if you want flowers to last much longer, they may be prepared by dissolving one teaspoon of gum arabic in 25ml (1fl. oz) of water or clear alcohol such as vodka. Then paint each petal with the mixture and proceed as from step 2 shown on this page. Flowers crystallised in this manner will keep for several months.

Crystallised flowers make very attractive winter decorations when fresh flowers are hard to find for cakes and may also be used for place or table settings.

Crystallised flowers are very fragile and should be handled with extreme care. For that reason, it is wise to crystallise extra flowers in case of breakage.

1 Mix 2 teaspoons cold water with 1 fresh egg white. Gently brush the flower petals with solution using soft, medium paint brush.

2 Sprinkle with caster sugar and shake off excess. Coat the back of the petals with the egg white and water solution.

3 Sprinkle with caster sugar. Place flowers on wire tray for 24 hours to dry.

CRYSTALLISING THROUGH THE SEASONS

SPRING	AUTUMN	Passionflower
Almond blossom	Clove pink	Pink
Apple blossom	Nasturtium	Rose
Chamomile	Pansy	Rosemary
Cherry blossom	Single Chrysanthemum	Scented Leaf
Daisy		Pelagonium
Heartsease	SUMMER	
Honeysuckle	Borage	WINTER
Japonica	Carnation	Jasmine
Lemon Balm	Chive	Freesia
Majoram	Cornflower	
Mint	Evening Primrose	
Pansy	Hibiscus	
Parsley	Honeysuckle	
Pear blossom	Hyssop	
Polyanthus	Jasmin	
Primula	Lavender	
Primrose	Lime Marigold	
Sage	Mimosa	
Violet	Nasturtium	

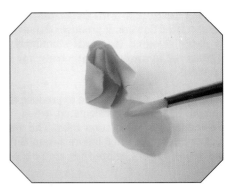

1 **To make a rose:** Mould a flower paste cone and fix to a length of wire with a little water. Cut out petal shape as shown, then thin the edges.

2 Thread the wire through the centre of the petals and wrap around the cone, fixing with a little cooled boiled water. Cut out a second set of petals and moisten.

3 Loosely fix the petals around the first petals to create a closed centre.

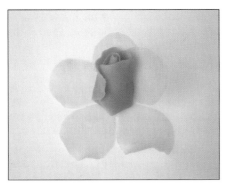

4 Repeat step 3 until the required size of rose is achieved.

5 Cut out calyx shape and then cut the edges as shown. Mould a cone.

6 Thread the wire through the calyx, then the cone and fix to the rose with a little water.

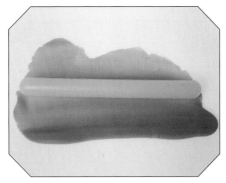

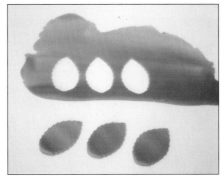

7 **To make wired leaves:** Roll flower paste to vary the thickness (thick at the base to thin at the tip of the leaves).

8 Cut out the leaves then vein with a veiner or mark with the back of a knife.

9 Thread wire, lightly moistened with water at the top, and push into the leaf. Tape together as required, with floral tape.

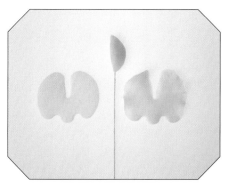

10 **To make a sweet pea:** Mould the shape shown with flower paste and fix to the wire, using a little water. Cut out, then frill the petals.

11 Fix the centre to the back of the petals as shown. Cut out, then frill a second set of petals.

12 Fix to the back of the flower. Tape the wire with floral tape. Wind taped wire around a cocktail stick to create tendrils and fix to the wire stem.

13 **To make a carnation:** Cut out the shape shown from flower paste, then frill the edge as shown.

14 Thread wire through the centre and fold in half, fixing with a little water. Fold together in three sections.

15 Repeat step 13. Thread the wire through the centre and fold round, fixing with a little water.

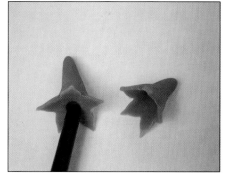

16 Mould a cone shape in the middle of a piece of flower paste. Thin out the edge, then cut out as shown.

17 Hollow the centre, using the end of a paint brush. Gently smooth and thin the edges.

18 Thread the wire through the calyx, then cut out and fix lower calyx, fixing with a little water. Colour with dusting powder or food colours.

1 Make wired pulled flowers, then tape together to form the sprays shown.

2 Make wired single sweet peas and sprays as shown.

3 Tape together a pulled flower spray, sweet pea spray and ribbon loops. 2 required.

4 Tape the single sweet peas to the sprays and then the pulled flower spray to one full spray.

5 Tape the sprays together to form the double ended spray as shown.

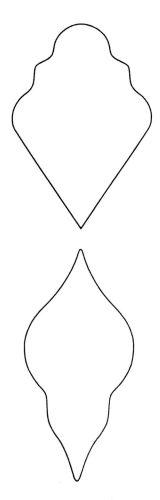

1 Using flower paste, mould a long pear shape onto 28 gauge wire, fixing with a little water, for the tongue. Cut out and shape with a modelling tool, the lower petal. Colour then fix to wire.

2 Using the template as a guide, cut out the petal shown, vein, frill around the sides, colour, then fix over the lower petal as shown, to form the throat.

3 Using the template as a guide, cut out and vein 5 petals. Frill 2 petals then fix all to single wires.

4 Tape the 3 unfrilled petals together, then the 3 frilled petals and finally the throat.

5 Make as many orchids as required, then tape together adding wired beads.

FLOWERS: PULLED

1 **To make pulled flowers:** Mould sugarpaste or flower paste into a cone. Hollow the centre using a cocktail stick. Cut edge into 5 sections.

2 Open out the petals, then thin the edges between finger and thumb.

3 Shape to the required size thinning each petal with a bone-shaped modelling tool.

4 For pointed petal-shaped flowers, follow steps 1 to 2, then squeeze each petal sideways. Thin to size required.

FLOWERS: SPRAY

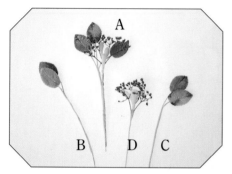

1 **To make a large floral spray:** Tape together 3 leaves, pulled flowers and dried gypsophila (A), 2 leaves (B), 2 leaves (C), then pulled flowers gypsophila (D).

2 Tape B, C and D to A. Tape 1 leaf (D), 1 leaf (E), then a rose bud, pulled flowers and gypsophila (F).

3 Tape D, E and F to A. Tape together pulled flowers and 2 leaves (G), pulled flowers and 2 leaves (H), then pulled flowers, carnation and gypsophila (J).

4 Tape G, H and J to A. Tape together pulled flowers, rose, 2 leaves and gypsophila (K), pulled flowers, carnation, 2 leaves and gypsophila (L), then pulled flowers, rose and gypsophila (M).

5 Tape K, L and M to A. Tape together 2 leaves, pulled flowers, carnation and gypsophila (N), 2 leaves, pulled flowers, carnation and gypsophila (P), then a rose and gypsophila (Q).

6 Tape N, P and Q to A. Adjust the flowers and leaves before adding more to the spray.

7 Picture shows the underside of the spray.

8 Tape together 4 leaves, 2 roses, carnation and gypsophila (R), then a rose, carnation, pulled flowers, 4 leaves and gypsophila (S).

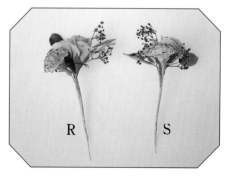

9 Side view of sprays made in step 8. Note how the flowers and leaves are taped together to form posy shapes.

GLOSSARY

Abbreviations

cm - centimetres
°C - degrees centigrade
°F - degrees farenheit
dsp - dessertspoon
g - gram
hrs - hours
in - inch
lbs - pounds
k - kilo
oz - ounces
lt - litre
mins - minutes
ml - millilitre
No. - piping tube number
pt - pint
tsp - teaspoon
tbsp - tablespoon

Broderie anglaise: An indented and piped pattern. See page 34.

Brushed embroidery: Icing brushed to resemble embroidery. See page 36.

Cake-base: Where the bottom edge of the cake meets the cake board.

Cake-card: A thin cake board.

Coated cake: A cake coated with buttercream or royal icing. See pages 58-60.

Collars: A runout fixed to the cake-top. See page 28.

Colouring: Colour may be added to pastes or icing at the mixing stage or painted on afterwards.

Covered cake: A cake covered with almond paste or sugarpaste. See pages 58-60.

Crimping: A design pressed into sugarpaste or almond paste.

Extension work: Supported or suspended piped lines. See page 79.

Figure piping: A figure piped with slightly softened royal icing (no glycerin) and without an outline. See page 139.

Filigree: Continuous irregular piped lines. See page 82.

Fix: to join.
  Almond paste to cake or cake to cake: apricot purée
  sugarpaste to sugarpaste: cooled boiled water
  Use royal icing to fix royal icing and modelling paste figures to cake.

Flood-in: Design piped within outline using royal icing without glycerin. See page 160, Runouts.

Flower paste: A fine sweet modelling paste used for delicate items. See page 89.

Frills: Fluted sugarpaste. See page 97.

Lace: Small piped pieces for attaching to cake. See page 112.

Lattice: Suspended piped lines in opposite directions to each other. See page 166.

Layer cakes: Cut and sandwich with filling of choice.

Leaf bag: A piping bag with the tip cut to a 'v' shape. See page 141.

Leave to dry: Leave for the time stated at a temperature of 18°C (65°F). Note: in high humidity a longer time may be needed.

Modelling paste: A strong paste used for cut out figures or a figure that stands alone. Fix to cake with royal icing. See page 120.

(No.1): Indicates piping tube number to be used. See page 143.

Non-stick paper: Specially prepared paper for figure piping and flood-in work.

Overpipe: To repeat the same pattern over existing piping.

Pipe-in: To pipe medium in use without a piping tube in the piping bag.

Pulled flowers: Small flowers moulded from a cone of paste using a cocktail stick and the fingers. See page 94.

Run-outs: Piped designs with an outline. See page 160.

Stippling: Royal icing stippled onto cake surface with a clean, dry, household sponge or palette knife.

Templates: An aid for designs. See page 178 and 184.

Tracery: A series of curves piped in clockwise and anti-clockwise directions.

Vein: To make the veins on a leaf, use a cocktail stick, back of a knife or a veiner. Cut with appropriate cutter or cardboard template.

Wiring flowers and leaves: Never insert wires directly into a cake. See page 90 onwards.

GOLDEN WEDDING

1 Outline and flood-in a figure 50. Leave until dry. Cover the cake and board with sugarpaste. Crimp the cake-top edge, side, base and board edge. Pipe shells with royal icing, around the cake-base (No.43).

2 Pipe a line over the shells (No.2) then overpipe the No.2 line (No.1). Pipe a decorative pattern around the edge of the board (No.1).

3 Paint the figure 50. Fix to the cake-top and decorate as shown. (See page 93 for orchid).

20.5cm round cake (8in)
680g almond paste (1½lb)
680g sugarpaste (1½lb)
225g royal icing (8oz)
Assorted food colours

28cm round cake board (11in)
Crimpers
Piping tubes No.1, 2 and 43
Non-stick paper
Fine paint brush

Flowers of choice
Board edge ribbon

See: Crimping
Runouts

GRANDMA

INGREDIENTS

20.5cm petal shaped cake (8in)
680g almond paste (1½lb)
1.5k sugarpaste (3lb)
115g royal icing (4oz)
85g flower paste (3oz)
Assorted food colours

EQUIPMENT and DECORATIONS

28cm petal shaped cake board (11in)
Frill cutter
Oval cutter
Cocktail stick
Piping tube No.1

Floral sprays
Ribbon bows
Board edge ribbon

See: Flowers
Frills

1 Cover the cake and board with thin sugarpaste. Moisten area covering the cake with cooled, boiled water leaving the petal ovals dry. Cover the cake with sugarpaste again, then cut and remove ovals as shown.

2 Make and fix a sugarpaste frill around the cake-base. Pipe shells along the top edge of the frill with royal icing (No.1).

3 Cut out and fix sugarpaste frills to the edge of the ovals. Decorate the cake with appropriate floral sprays and ribbons as required.

HALLOWEEN

INGREDIENTS

25.5cm hexagonal shaped cake (10in)
1.25k almond paste (2½lb)
2k sugarpaste (4lb)
115g royal icing (4oz)
Assorted food colours

EQUIPMENT and DECORATIONS

35.5cm hexagonal cake board (14in)
Fine paint brush
Piping tube No.1
Board edge ribbon

1 Cover the cake and board with
sugarpaste. Using the template as
a guide, cut out and fix a
sugarpaste ghost to the cake-top.

2 Cut out and fix a second ghost,
then paint in their faces.

3 Cut out and paint a selection of
sugarpaste figures and shapes.

4 Fix to the cake-side with cut-out
moons and stars. Pipe spiders
webs onto the board with royal
icing (No.1). Pipe inscription of
choice onto the cake-top (No.1).

HINTS and TIPS

ALMOND PASTE

Almond paste differs from marzipan in that almond paste is a mixture of uncooked ground almonds, sugar and eggs. Marzipan is a mixture of cooked ground almonds and sugar.
All equipment should be thoroughly clean.
Only use best quality ground almonds.
Do not overmix as oil will be squeezed from the almonds and ruin the paste.
Under no circumstances should flour come into contact with almond paste.
Store almond paste in polythene bags in a cool, dry place.
If paste is too hard for use, wrap in greaseproof paper and gently warm until pliable.
When rolling almond paste use icing or caster sugar for dusting. Ensure the almond paste on a cake has a level top and vertical sides.
Boiling apricot purée is the most appropriate fixing agent.
As almond paste forms a barrier between the cake and the royal icing, it should be of sufficient thickness to prevent discolouration.
Leave almond paste covered cake to dry for three to four days in a dry room.
Do not store almond paste in a sealed plastic container.

ALBUMEN SOLUTION

It is essential that all utensils are completely free from grease and sterilised in boiling water. Albumen solution should only be made from pure dried egg white and water.
Pure albumen powder will keep indefinitely if stored in a cool dry place in a sealed container. Only use cold water as warm water may cook the albumen.
Made up solution will keep several days in a sealed container in a refrigerator.
Albumen solution goes very lumpy when first mixed.

BUTTERCREAM

To obtain best results, always use best fresh butter and sifted icing sugar.
If buttercream is too dense, continue beating until a light fluffy texture is reached.
Ensure buttercream is at room temperature before use.

CURDLING

Curdling of sponge or cake mixes can occur if eggs are added too quickly or if there is insufficient beating between additions. If curdling does occur, immediately beat in a small amount of flour until batter is smooth.

FREEZING

Sponges can be frozen for up to six months.

FRUIT CAKE

Too hot an oven will produce a cracked crusted top and uncooked centre with burnt fruit around crust.
Too cool an oven will produce a pale, thick crust with uncooked fruit. It will not keep and may go mouldy.
If a cake has been baked at correct temperature but sinks in the middle, there could be too much liquid in the batter, baking powder, sugar or fat.
If cake is crumbly, cause may be curdled batter, overbeating the fat, sugar and eggs, undermixing the flour and fruit into batter, insufficient sugar.
See Wedding Cake.

PIPING GEL

Use a small piping bag and do not overfill.
Outline each section in royal icing before filling with piping gel if required.

PORTIONS

A 20.5cm (8in) round sponge provides about 16 portions. A 20.5cm (8in) round fruit cake provides about 40 portions and a square cake 54 portions.

ROYAL ICING

Never coat a cake with royal icing unless icing has been standing for 24 hours.
Always stir the royal icing before coating a cake. Ensure cake is correctly placed on board before coating commences.
Only use non-ferrous tools for royal icing.
Apply at least three royal icing coatings.
Each coating should be allowed to dry before applying the next.
Before adding a further coat of royal icing, make sure the previous coating has been trimmed smooth. Do not dip palette knife or ruler into water when applying royal icing.
Stir a drop of cold water into royal icing which is too stiff to easily coat a cake.
Royal icing for figure piping and runouts should be made with pure albumen powder.
Make royal icing for figure piping and runouts 24 hours before use.
Icing for figure piping should be soft but firm enough to hold its shape.
Plan each stage of a piped figure. Each stage must be joined to another with no gaps.
Use small piping bags for figure piping.
Increase pressure on the piping bag to build up face features or contours.

Royal icing for runouts should should have sufficient water to achieve a dropping consistency but too much water will prevent the runout from setting.
Use good quality waxed paper or non-stick paper for runouts. It should be as smooth and transparent as possible. If using waxed paper, ensure the runout is on the waxed side.
Before filling a piping bag with runout royal icing, tap the container on the table to expel air bubbles.
A piped runout outline must be complete.
In periods of high humidity, longer drying times may be necessary.
Although runouts can be made ahead of time, they must be stored in a cardboard box in a dry and warm place.

SPONGE CAKE

A too hot an oven will produce a sponge of poor volume which is highly crusted and coloured. The centre may be uncooked with numerous holes.
Too cool an oven will produce a pale sponge which is coarse with a thick crust. It will go stale very quickly.
Do not allow mixture to settle on the sides of the mixing bowl as streaking will occur in finished sponge.
Do not knock or drop the cake tin when filled with batter.

SUGARPASTE

All utensils must be scrupulously clean.
Sugarpaste must be made 24 hours before use.
Ready made sugarpaste can be purchased from supermarkets and specialist suppliers. If the sugarpaste is found to be dry, add a little white fat or egg-white to the mixture.
If the sugarpaste is too sticky, a little cornflour or icing sugar can be added. Sugarpaste should be stored in an air-tight plastic container in a cool, dry place. Do not store in the refrigerator.
If sugarpaste has formed a crust, remove crust before use.

INGREDIENTS

20.5 x 10cm oblong sponge
  (8 x 4in) 2 required
680g sugarpaste (1½lb)
115g royal icing (4oz)
Dusting powder
Assorted food colours

EQUIPMENT and DECORATIONS

25.5 x 20.5cm oblong cake board
  (10 x 8in)
Decorative board covering
Fine paint brush
Piping tube No.1

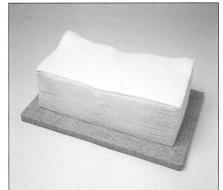

1 Layer the sponges together and cover with sugarpaste. Mark the sides with the back of a knife. Cut out and fix a piece of sugarpaste to the cake-top, leaving the edges slightly raised.

2 Cut out a second sheet of sugarpaste and leave to dry over an uneven surface. When dry, paint the design of a bank note then lightly brush with dusting powder. Fix to the cake-top. Cut out and fix a sugarpaste band. Pipe inscription of choice with royal icing (No.1).

INGREDIENTS

15cm round sponge (6in)
 3 required
25.5cm round sponge (10in)
 3 required
3 small swiss rolls
2.5k sugarpaste (5lb)
225g royal icing (8oz)
Assorted food colours

EQUIPMENT and DECORATIONS

35.5cm oval cake board (14in)
Ruler
Coarse cloth
Fluted cutter
Blossom cutter
Ice-cream cones or cardboard
Fine sponge
Leaf piping bag
Decorations
Board edge ribbon

1 Layer the three large sponges together with filling of choice. Cover with sugarpaste. Mark with a coarse cloth, then mark the lines shown with a ruler. Repeat for the small sponges.

Cake decorating is a challenge to your ingenuity. Many simple, everyday items can be used to create exciting cakes. Everything should be edible or food approved, unless used for items that are purely for decoration. Small cake cards are useful to place between non-food approved material and the cake itself.

Many decorative items can be created from what you already have in your kitchen or toy cupboard. But, a trip round your local supermarket, newsagents, or confectioners may well produce other ideas.

Sweets, biscuits and liquorice shapes have an obvious decorating appeal. But, you can also use breakfast cereals or coloured sugars, nuts and coconut to create a variety of effects. Chocolate is extremely versatile. It can be grated, broken or piped. Many newsagents sell stencils and decorative papers to excite your imagination.

In the cake shown here, ice-cream cones have been used but empty yogurt pots, shaped cardboard or other containers could be adapted as necessary. Rice paper can be rolled, folded or otherwise shaped – especially if dampened and moulded. The pastry cutters you have in your kitchen can be extremely useful, but bottle tops and many other items can double as cutters if necessary.

Texture is an important feature on many novelty cakes. A cheese grater offers several possibilities. Forks, sieves and coarse materials can also be utilised.

2 Cut out and fix sugarpaste ramparts, windows and doors to each sponge. Cut the swiss rolls to various lengths. Cover each piece with sugarpaste, mark with the coarse cloth then mark the lines.

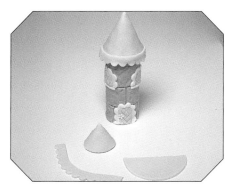

3 Cover ice-cream cones, or cardboard cones, with sugarpaste and fix. Cut out and fix sugarpaste windows and doors.

4 Fix the large and small sponges onto the board. Stipple the remaining surface with royal icing then fix the turrets.

5 Pipe a creeping plant over the castle, with royal icing, using a leaf shaped piping bag. Fix decorations of choice.

JACK-IN-THE-BOX

INGREDIENTS

15cm square sponge (6in)
4 required
1 large swiss roll
900g sugarpaste (2lb)
115g royal icing (4oz)
Assorted food colours

EQUIPMENT and DECORATIONS

25.5cm square cake board (10in)
Decorative board covering
15cm cake card (6in) 2 required
Small round cutters

Cocktail stick
Piping tubes No.1, 2 and 7
Dowelling
Paper hat and wand

1 Cover the board with decorative paper. Layer the sponges together then cover with sugarpaste. Fix to cake card, then to the board. Fix three-quarters of the swiss roll onto the cake-top.

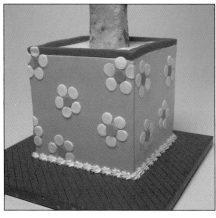

2 Cut out and fix sugarpaste circles to the cake-side to form flower shapes. Pipe shells around the cake-base with royal icing (No.7).

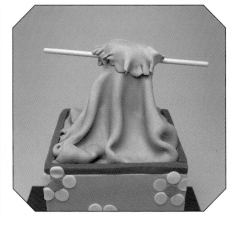

3 Roll out mottled coloured sugarpaste and drape over the swiss roll to form the coat. Fix dowelling across the top and cover with a fluted piece of sugarpaste for the collar.

4 Make and fix sugarpaste sleeves and hands as shown.

5 Cover the remaining quarter of Swiss roll with sugarpaste and decorate as shown for the head. Fix to the collar.

6 Cover the cake card with sugarpaste and fix to the cake-top edge for the lid. Pipe shells around the edge (No.2). Fix the hat, then cut and fix sugarpaste hair. Fix the wand.

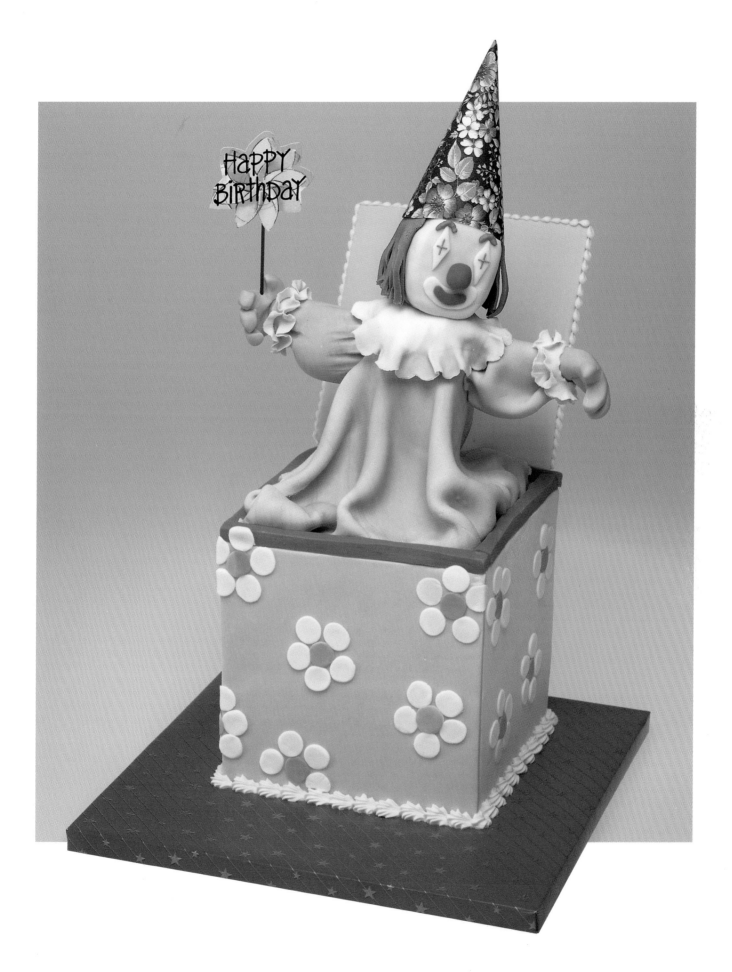

INGREDIENTS

20.5cm square cake (8in)
900g almond paste (2lb)
1.25g royal icing (2½lb)
Assorted food colours

EQUIPMENT and DECORATIONS

25.5cm square cake board (10in)
Non-stick paper
Piping tube No.1
Assorted cake decorations
Board edge ribbon

See: Runouts

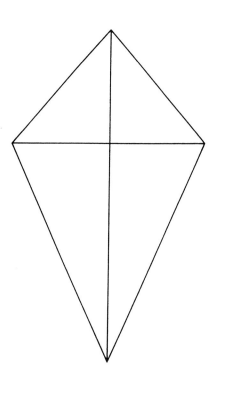

1 Coat the cake with royal icing. For the final coating use mottled coloured royal icing for the cake-top and then stipple the cake-sides and board as shown. Leave until dry.

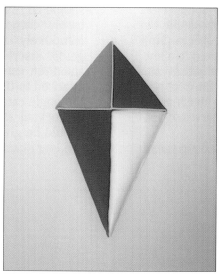

2 Outline (No.1) and flood-in the kites onto non-stick paper using royal icing. 4 required. Leave to dry for 24 hours. Pipe the various lines shown (No.1).

3 Pipe inscription of choice and string lines as shown (No.1).

4 Soften a little royal icing and pipe-in the clouds on the cake-top between the lines.

5 Overpipe the lines in a variety of colours (No.1). Fix the kites to the cake-top. Fix decorations around the cake board.

MADEIRA CAKE

For hexagonal, octagonal or petal shaped madeira cakes use recipe for the equivalent round cake. Example, for 20.5cm (8in) heart shape use ingredients for 20.5cm (8in) round cake.

Square tin	12.5cm (5in)	15cm (6in)	18cm (7in)	20.5cm (8in)	23cm (9in)	25.5cm (10in)	28cm (11in)
OR							
Round tin	15cm (6in)	18cm (7in)	20.5cm (8in)	23cm (9in)	25.5cm (10in)	28cm (11in)	30.5cm (12in)
Butter	60g (2oz)	115g (4oz)	170g (6oz)	225g (8oz)	285g (10oz)	340g (12oz)	400g (14oz)
Caster sugar	60g (2oz)	115g (4oz)	170g (6oz)	225g (8oz)	285g (10oz)	340g (12oz)	400g (14oz)
Eggs, size 2	1	2	3	4	5	6	7
Plain flour	30g (1oz)	60g (2oz)	85g (3oz)	115g (4oz)	145g (5oz)	170g (6oz)	200g (7oz)
Self-raising flour	60g (2oz)	115g (4oz)	170g (6oz)	225g (8oz)	285g (10oz)	340g (12oz)	400g (14oz)
Lemons	¼	½	1	1	1½	1½	2
Baking temperature	--------170°C (325°F) or Gas Mark 3--------						
Approximate baking time	¾hr	1hr	1¼hrs	1¼hrs	1¼hrs	1½hrs	1½hrs

BAKING TEST Bring the cake forward in the oven at the end of the recommended baking time so that it can be tested. Insert a stainless steel skewer into the centre of the cake and slowly withdraw it. If the cake is sufficiently baked, the skewer will come out of the cake as cleanly as it went in. Continue baking at the same temperature if the cake mixture clings to the skewer. Test every ten minutes until the skewer is clean when withdrawn from the cake.

STORAGE When cold, madeira can be deep frozen for up to six months. Use within three days of baking or defrosting.

PORTIONS A 20.5cm (8in) round madeira cake should serve approximately sixteen portions when decorated.

INGREDIENTS

170g butter (6oz)
170g caster sugar (6oz)
3 eggs, size 2
85g plain flour (3oz)
170g self raising flour (6oz)
1 lemon

EQUIPMENT

18cm square cake tin (7in)
OR
20.5cm round cake tin (8in)
Greaseproof paper
Mixing bowl
Mixing spoon
Spatula

BAKING

Bake in a pre-heated oven at 170°C (325°F) or Gas Mark 3 for 1¼hrs.

1 Grease the tin lightly with butter, fully line with greaseproof paper, then grease the paper.

2 Cream the butter and sugar together until light and fluffy.

3 Stir the egg(s) together before beating a little at a time into the creamed mixture (see curdling).

4 Lightly fold the sifted flours into the mixture together with the lemon rind and juice.

5 Place mixture into the tin, and using a spatula, level the top. Bake for recommended time.

6 See baking test instructions. When baked, leave in the tin to cool for 10 minutes before turning out onto a wire rack to cool completely.

MELTING CHOCOLATE

Chocolate flavoured cake covering has almost all the cocoa butter content replaced with vegetable fat. It is readily available in supermarkets as blocks of plain, milk or white varieties. It produces a smooth, glossy cake coating suitable for children or adults. A whole range of design possibilities are opened up by colouring white chocolate flavoured cake covering with powder colours.

The method shown here is a quick and easy way to melt chocolate flavoured cake covering. A double-boiler saucepan should ideally be used as this prevents scorching, but alternatively a heat-proof bowl can be used over an ordinary saucepan which is small enough to support the bowl without it touching the base. The water level should not be allowed to touch the bowl.

PIPING CHOCOLATE: Use a small amount at a time and keep the remainder warm when not in use.

1 Working in a cool room temperature, place broken pieces into a heat-proof bowl.

2 Stand the bowl over a pan of simmering, not boiling, water and stir until the chocolate is almost melted.

3 Remove from the heat and continue stirring until chocolate is smooth and completely melted. Keep it warm, stirring occasionally, to prevent it from setting while in use.

MODELLING CHARACTERS

INGREDIENTS

25.5 x 20.5cm cake (10 x 8in)
1.25k almond paste (2½lb) for the cake
680g almond paste (1½lb) for the figures
2k sugarpaste (4lb)
225g royal icing (8oz)
Red dusting powder
Assorted food colours

EQUIPMENT and DECORATIONS

35.5 x 25.5cm cake board (14 x 10in)
40.5 x 35.5cm cake board (16 x 14in)
Modelling tools
Dowelling
Fine paint brush
Cocktail stick

Piping tubes No.1 and 2
Dragees
Small parcels
Ribbon
Board edge ribbon

1 Fix the boards together then cover the cake and boards with mottled coloured sugarpaste. Fix ribbon around the cake-base and board edge. Leave to dry.

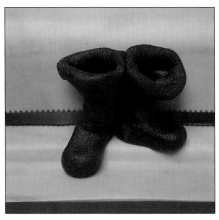

2 Use almond paste for Father Christmas and elves. Mould the boots and fix to the front of the cake as shown.

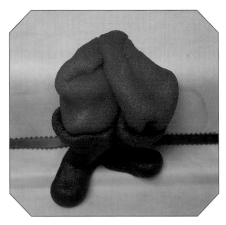

3 Mould and shape the trouser legs and fix into the boot.

4 Mould a large piece into a body and jacket and fix to the trousers. Pipe rope line around the edge with royal icing (No.2).

5 Mould and decorate the head (following the basic instructions for elves heads) and fix to the body using a cocktail stick for support.

6 Mould and fix hat, arms and gloves. Decorate with royal icing as shown.

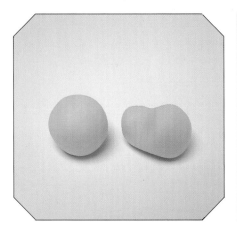

7 To make an elves head, first mould almond paste into a ball then to a wide pear shape.

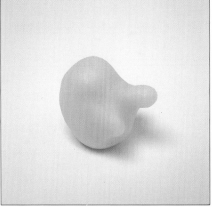

8 Pinch out the nose and cheeks and slightly indent for the eyes.

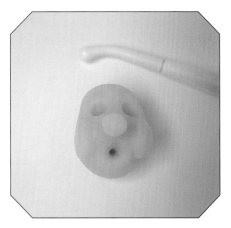

9 Using a modelling tool, indent the eyes to required depth, then form an open mouth.

118

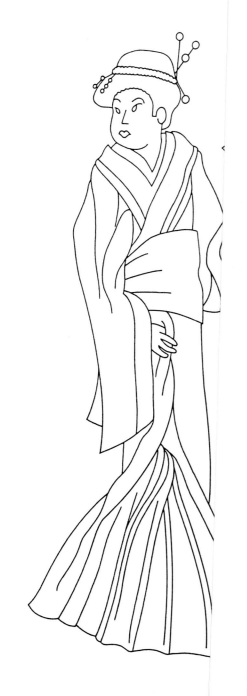

 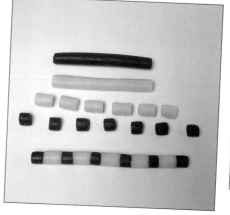 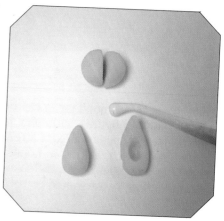

10 Make and fix ears. Brush the cheeks with dusting powder. Pipe in the eyes with royal icing then pipe the lips (No.1).

11 For the legs, roll two colours of almond paste. Cut into long and short lengths as shown, then join together.

12 For the shoes, mould almond paste into a small ball. Cut in half and mould into pear shape. Using a modelling tool, indent as shown.

13 Fold the legs over and fix on the shoes. Mould the body, using a dowel to hollow out the base.

14 Cut the edge in a zig-zag pattern and fix to the legs.

15 Mould and fix arms and hands as shown.

16 Fix on the head. Make and fix a hat, then decorate with piped royal icing and a silver dragee. Repeat steps 7 to 16 for the additional elf as shown.

17 Repeat steps 7 to 16 for two more elves in various positions and shapes.

18 Repeat steps 7 to 16 for two more elves in various positions and shapes. Fix to the cake as required. Then decorate with small parcels.

119

1 Cover the board with decorative paper. Cover the cake with sugarpaste and leave to dry. Using the template as a guide, mould body of the lady from modelling paste and fix to the cake-top.

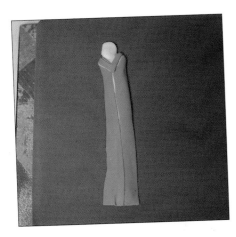

2 Roll out modelling paste very thinly, cut and fix to the body as shown.

3 Cut out a square piece of modelling paste, fold and gather at the top to form a triangular shape and fix to the base. Cut and fix top pieces.

4 Cut
flow

MOTHER

INGREDIENTS

20.5cm round cake (8in)
680g almond paste (1½lb)
900g sugarpaste (2lb)
225g royal icing (8oz)
Pink and spearmint green food
 colours

EQUIPMENT and DECORATIONS

28cm round cake board (11in)
Piping tube No.1
Non-stick paper
Small blossom cutter
Feathers

Narrow ribbon
Bows
Board edge ribbon

See: Lace

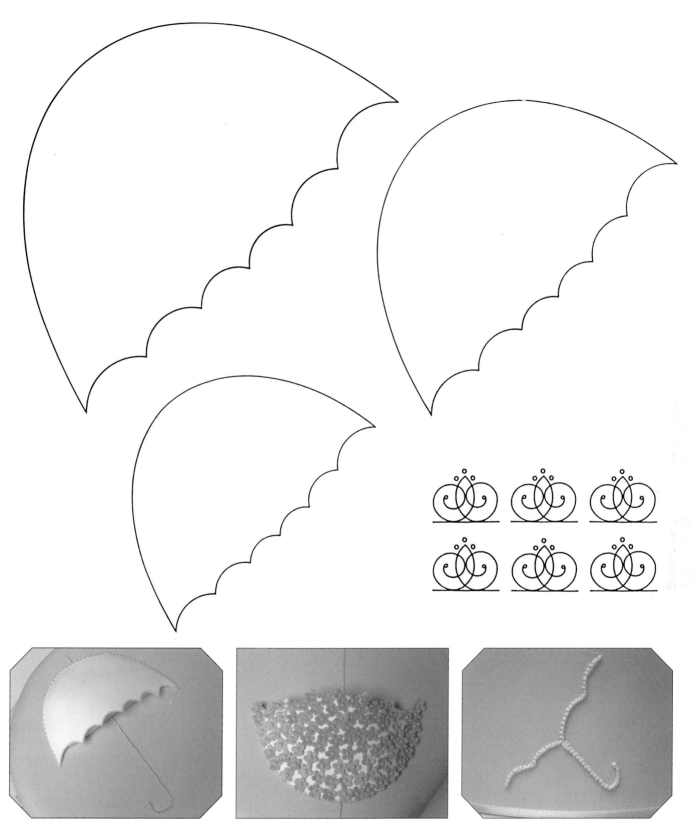

1 Cover the cake with sugarpaste. Fix to the board. Coat board with royal icing. Pipe 50 lace pieces (No.1) onto non-stick paper. Make and fix sugarpaste umbrella. Pipe dots and rope handle (No.1).

2 Cut out and fix miniature sugarpaste blossoms. Pipe a dot in each centre (No.1). Fix narrow ribbon around the cake-base. Divide the cake-side into six sections. Pipe opposing umbrella frames with a rope line (No.1).

3 Decorate with miniature blossoms. pipe bows, inscription of choice and tracery (No.1). Fix the lace pieces around the cake-top edge when dry.

MOTHER'S DAY

INGREDIENTS

20.5cm heart shaped cake (8in)
680g almond paste (1½lb)
1.25k royal icing (2½lb)
115g sugarpaste (4oz)
Blue, green and peach food
  colours

EQUIPMENT and DECORATIONS

30.5cm heart shaped cake board (12in)
Non-stick paper
Piping tubes No.1, 2 and 43
Miniature blossom cutter

Board edge ribbon

See: Runouts
      Flowers

1 Coat the cake and board with royal icing. Using the template as a guide, outline and flood-in the cake-top runout onto non-stick paper (No.1). When dry, pipe the dots shown.

2 Outline and flood-in the board run-out. When dry, pipe shells around the cake-base (No.43). Pipe the dots shown (No.1). Pipe stalks around the cake-side (No.1).

3 Pipe leaves onto the stalks using a leaf bag. Cut-out and fix miniature sugarpaste blossoms as shown. Pipe a dot in each centre (No.1).

4 Carefully remove the run-out from the non-stick paper and fix to the cake-top.

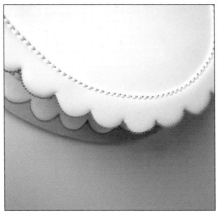

5 Pipe shells around the inside edge of the run-out (No.2). Pipe a dot between each shell (No.1).

6 Pipe stalks and leaves onto the cake-top and decorate with miniature sugarpaste blossoms. Pipe inscription of choice (No.1).

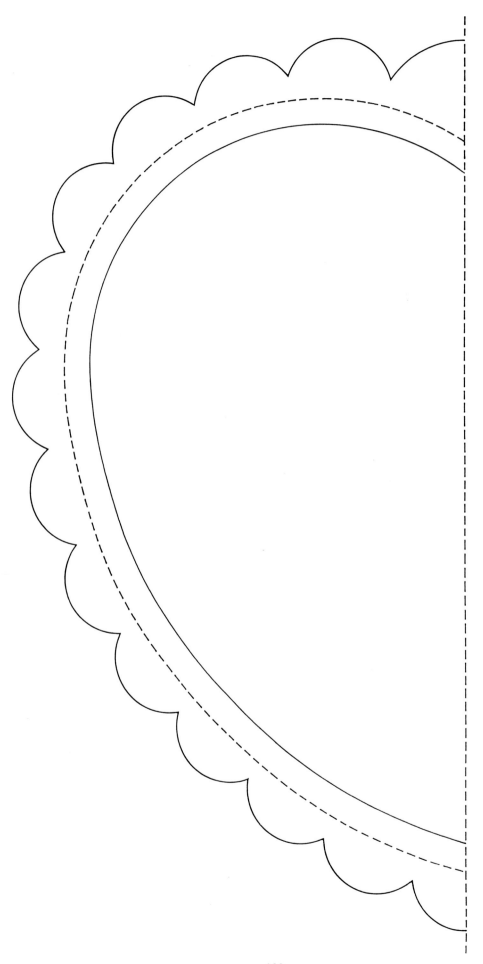

128

INGREDIENTS

Sponge baked in a 1.2Lt pudding
  basin (2pt) 2 required
900g sugarpaste (2lb)
115g royal icing (4oz)
Assorted food colours

EQUIPMENT and DECORATIONS

30.5cm round cake board (12in)
Support for cake
Piping tube No.1
Decorative flowers
Board edge ribbon

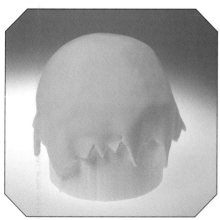

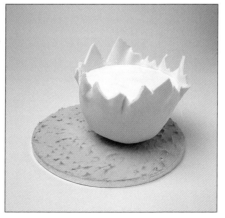

1 Place one sponge onto a support, then cover with sugarpaste. Trim the side to give a broken shell effect. Leave until firm to the touch.

2 When the sugarpaste is firm, stipple the board with royal icing, upturn the sponge from the support and fix to the icing. Then cut out and fix a sugarpaste top.

3 Cover the remaining sponge with sugarpaste and decorate as shown. Fix onto the shell. Decorate the board with flowers and sugarpaste plaque. Pipe inscription of choice with royal icing (No.1).

NOVELTY HELMET

INGREDIENTS

Sponge baked in a 1.2Lt pudding
 basin (2pt)
900g sugarpaste (2lb)
115g royal icing (4oz)
Assorted food colours

EQUIPMENT and DECORATIONS

30.5cm round cake board (12in)
Leaf cutters
Fine paint brush
Modelling tools
Piping tube No.1
Board edge ribbon

1 Roughly spread two colours of royal icing onto the board, using a palette knife, to create the ground. Cover the sponge with sugarpaste and place onto the board.

2 Roll sugarpaste into lengths and fix over the helmet as shown.

3 Roll varying colours of sugarpaste together, then cut out a selection of leaf shapes and fix as shown.

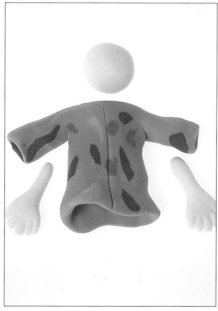

4 Mould a piece of sugarpaste, fix various colours to it, then mould again to form the camouflage material.

5 Mould the body, hands and head.

6 Mould the legs and fix into the body, then mould the boots and fix. Position as required, then fix remaining pieces. Paint the faces. Pipe inscription of choice (No.1).

PAINTING

Painting on a cake is a wonderful opportunity to allow your artistic talent to shine. It is worked on a sugarpaste or royal iced cake that has been allowed to dry thoroughly. Inspiration can be found on cards or photographs according to the occasion and interests of the recipient.

Always practice first.

Transfer the design to the cake as lightly as possible. When painting, use a fine paint brush. Start with the background and work pale colours to deep colours. The colours should not be too weak as they need to be applied thinly.

INGREDIENTS

20.5cm round cake (8in)
680g sugarpaste (1½lb)
680g almond paste (1½lb)
60g modelling paste (2oz)
155g royal icing (4oz)
Clear alcohol
Assorted food colours

EQUIPMENT and DECORATIONS

28cm round cake board (11in)
Crimper
Fine paint brush
Piping tube No.1
Board edge ribbon

See: Transferring designs

1 Cover the board with sugarpaste, then cover the cake with sugarpaste and fix to the board. Leave until dry. Transfer the template onto the cake-top. Dilute colours with clear alcohol and brush-in the colours shown.

2 Using stronger diluted colours, brush-in the second layer of colours shown.

3 Using slightly diluted colours brush-in the final colours to create the picture shown.

4 Roll out a long strip of modelling paste and fix around the cake-base to form ribbon and bows.

5 Repeat step 4, onto the cake-top edge. Cut out and fix heart shapes. Pipe dotted lines, then inscription of choice with royal icing (No.1).

PIPING

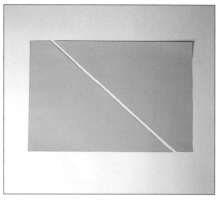

1 To make a piping bag: Cut a sheet of greaseproof paper 20.5 x 30.5cm (8 x 12in).

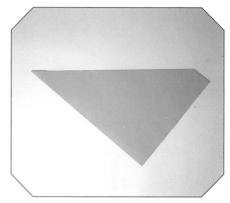

2 Cut the sheet diagonally as shown.

3 Turn one triangle to position shown.

4 Using right hand, curl the right corner of the paper towards the centre.

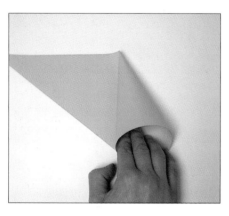

5 Continue curling the paper, as shown.

6 Using left hand, bring left-hand corner of the paper over to the right.

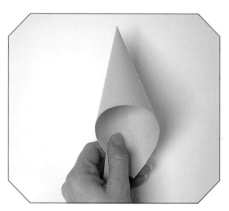

7 Continue by curling the paper under the cone.

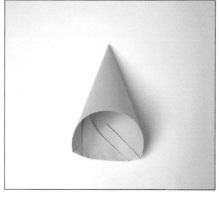

8 Fold and crease ends into the cone.

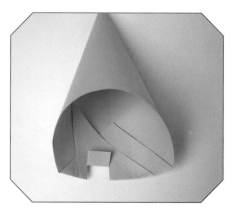

9 Make two cuts and fold paper inwards to secure the piping bag.

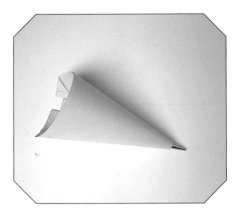

10 Cut the tip off the piping bag and drop in a piping tube.

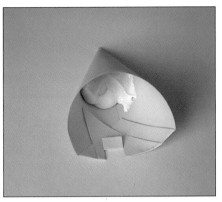

11 To fill the piping bag: Using a palette knife, half fill the piping bag with royal icing.

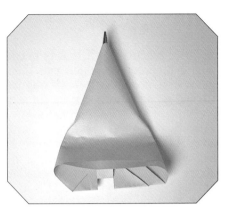

12 Flatten the wide opening of the piping bag, gently squeezing the icing towards the piping tube.

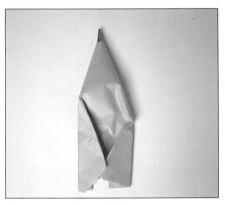

13 Fold each side of the piping bag to the centre.

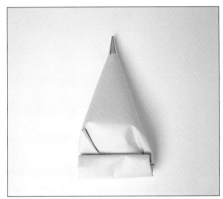

14 Roll the wide end of the piping bag towards the piping tube to secure.

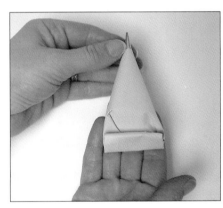

15 To hold a piping bag for writing: Place the piping bag onto the tips of your fingers.

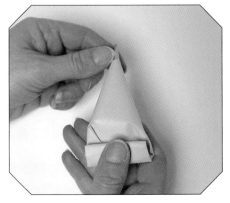

16 Now place your thumb against the rolled end.

17 Prepare to use the piping bag for piping as shown.

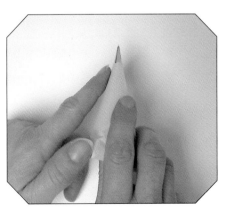

18 Turn your hand over so that the first finger is in line with the piping tube.

PIPING: BORDERS

Piping borders is an opportunity to use your ingenuity and develop your design skill.

Once the basic piped shapes have been mastered, the different forms can be used to create a cake to suit a particular occasion, or the personality and age of the recipient.

As can be seen from the pictures below, simple changes to the border subtly alter the mood of a cake. It can become more formal, or softer; imaginative or traditional; appropriate for a wedding, or a christening, a birthday or a retirement.

PIPING: FIGURES

Quick and easy decorations for cakes, piped figures need little expertise.

Royal icing without glycerin, of a soft peaking consistency which holds its shape, should be used. Pipe onto clear, non-stick paper placed over a template. Increase pressure to build up features and contours where appropriate. Thin paper allows for easy removal once the icing is dry.

Leave piped figures in a warm place to dry.

1 Use royal icing made 24 hours before. Place in a small bowl and soften with a drop of cold water. Colour small amounts of royal icing by mixing on a tile with a palette knife.

2 Make sufficient small piping bags for the required colours, then fill each with a different colour. Cut a small tip off each piping bag.

3 Draw the required design (template) on paper, secure on a tile or flat surface, then overlay and fix non-stick paper.

4 Pipe-in the face, ensuring that the cheeks and nose are thicker and eyes more shallow. Then pipe-in the hands. Leave to dry for 10 minutes.

5 Pipe-in the arms and shoes. Leave to dry for 10 minutes.

6 Pipe-in the remaining parts of the body. Leave to dry for 10 minutes.

7 Pipe-in the ruff, then the hair and finally the hat. Leave to dry for 24 hours.

8 When completely dry paint the dots and face with food colours, then pipe the dots shown. Remove from the non-stick paper when required.

PIPING: FLOWERS and LEAVES

Note: Use royal icing without glycerin.

1 **PIPED FLOWERS.** Fix waxed or non-stick paper to top of flower nail.

2 Turn nail whilst piping through a petal shaped piping tube to form each petal. When complete, leave until dry.

3 **PIPED LEAVES.** Mark, then cut tip off piping bag where indicated.

4 Pipe leaves to required size.

SEQUENCE SHOWING BASIC PIPED FLOWER

VIOLET

ROSE

SWEET PEA

PIPING: SHAPES

Note: Any star or plain piping tube can be used.

1 STAR. Hold piping bag still in a vertical position and press.

2 At required size, stop pressing and lift bag upright.

3 ROSETTE. Press upright bag whilst turning in a clockwise motion.

4 On completion of one turn stop pressing and draw bag away.

5 'C' LINE. Pipe in anti-clockwise and upwards direction.

6 Form tail, stop piping and slide tube on surface.

7 LATERAL 'C' LINE. Pipe in anti-clockwise direction at an even height to form first curve.

8 Continue piping to form the matching curve. Stop piping and lift bag upright.

9 SKEIN. Pipe in anti-clockwise direction at an even height to form the first curve.

10 Continue piping in clockwise direction to form matching curve. Stop piping and lift bag upright.

11 REVERSE SKEIN. Pipe in a clockwise direction at an even height to form the first curve.

12 Continue piping in anti-clockwise direction and stop when the matching opposite curve is complete, then lift bag upright.

13 SHELL. Hold piping bag at the angle shown and start to press.

14 Continue pressing whilst lifting the bag.

15 Continue pressing until required size.

16 Stop pressing, then slide tube down along surface to form tail.

17 ZIGZAG LINE. Pipe in tight waves whilst keeping tube on surface.

18 Continue piping an even zigzag. Stop piping and slide tube away.

19 ROPE. Pipe spring shape in clockwise direction, using even pressure and keeping bag horizontal.

20 Continue piping in a straight even pattern. Stop piping and pull bag away in half-turn.

21 CONVEX ROPE. Pipe-spring shape in clockwise direction, using even pressure and keeping bag horizontal.

22 Continue piping to form the curve shown. Stop piping and pull bag away in a half-turn.

23 CONCAVE ROPE. Pipe spring-shape in clockwise direction, using even pressure and keeping bag horizontal.

24 Continue piping to form the curve shown. Stop piping and pull bag away in a half-turn.

25 SPIRAL SHELL. Hold piping bag at the angle shown and start to press.

26 Continue piping in clockwise direction, increasing the size of the circle with each turn.

27 Continue piping in clockwise direction but, from the centre, decrease the size of the circle with each turn.

28 To complete spiral shell, stop piping and pull bag away in a half-turn.

29 'C' SCROLL. Pipe in clockwise direction, increasing the size of the circle to form the body.

30 Continue piping, reducing the size of the circles, then form the tail using reduced pressure.

31 REVERSE 'C' SCROLL. Pipe in a clockwise direction, increasing the size of the circle to form the body.

32 Continue piping, reducing the size of the circles, then form the tail using reduced pressure.

33 'S' SCROLL. piping bag at angle shown and start to press.

34 Continue piping in a clockwise direction, increasing the size of each circle to form the body.

35 Continue piping, reducing the size of the circles from the centre.

36 Continue piping and form the tail by reducing pressure.

37 REVERSED 'S' SCROLL. piping bag at angle shown and start to press.

38 Continue piping in an anti-clockwise direction, increasing the size of each circle to form the body.

39 Continue piping, reducing the size of the circles from the centre.

40 Continue piping and form the tail by reducing the pressure.

PIPING: TUBES and SHAPES

PIPING TUBES

The diagram shows the icing tube shapes used in this book. Please note that these are Mary Ford tubes, but comparable tubes may be used.

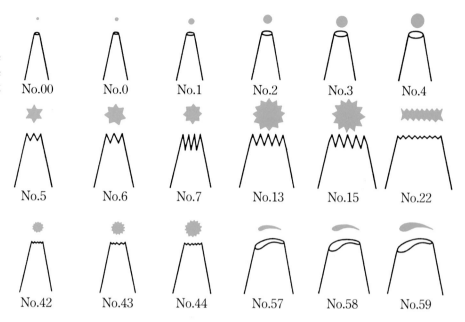

No.00 No.0 No.1 No.2 No.3 No.4

No.5 No.6 No.7 No.13 No.15 No.22

No.42 No.43 No.44 No.57 No.58 No.59

PIPING GEL

INGREDIENTS

20.5cm round cake (8in)
680g almond paste (1½lb)
900g sugarpaste (2lb)
115g piping gel (4oz)
115g royal icing (4oz)
Assorted food colours

EQUIPMENT and DECORATIONS

28cm round cake board (11in)
Crimper
Fine paint brush
Piping tube No.1
Narrow ribbon
Board edge ribbon

Many supermarkets now stock tubes of clear or coloured piping gel. Clear gel can be coloured with liquid or paste food colours as required.

Use a small piping bag without a tube for each colour to be piped. Do not overfill the bag as a little piping gel can go a very long way. Outline each section with royal icing before filling with piping gel if required. There is no need to wait for the previous section to dry before moving onto the next.

RECIPE

INGREDIENTS

60g fresh lemon juice (2fl. oz)
20ml cornflour (1 rounded tbsp)
60g water (2fl. oz)
60g caster sugar (4tbsp)

Place all ingredients into a small saucepan and dissolve over low heat, stirring continually until boiled and thick. Remove from the heat. If the mixture is too thick add a little water. Leave until cool. Colour as required. Store in a screw top jar in a refrigerator. This gel will not keep as long as commercial piping gel.

144

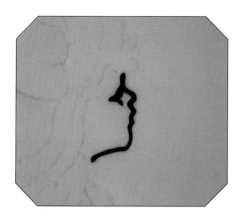

1 Cover the cake and board with sugarpaste, then crimp around the board edge. Leave until dry. Using the template as a guide, transfer the designs onto the cake-top and side. Pipe face line with royal icing. (No.1).

2 Pipe-in the figure with various colours of piping gel, using a piping bag without a piping tube.

3 Pipe the stalks and leaves as shown with piping gel.

4 Pipe a thick line around the edge of the large leaves and gently brush the gel towards the centres.

5 Pipe the berries with piping gel. Pipe inscription of choice onto the cake-top with royal icing (No.1). Pipe tracery, with piping gel, around the cake-top edge.

145

INGREDIENTS

25.5cm square sponge (10in)
900g sugarpaste (2lb)
115g royal icing (4oz)
Pink and blue food colours

EQUIPMENT and DECORATIONS

33cm round cake board (13in)
Decorative board covering
Modelling tools
Cake card

Piping tube No.1
Small decorations
Board edge ribbon

Crea
requi
cuts

Simp
anim
creat

You
and h
any e

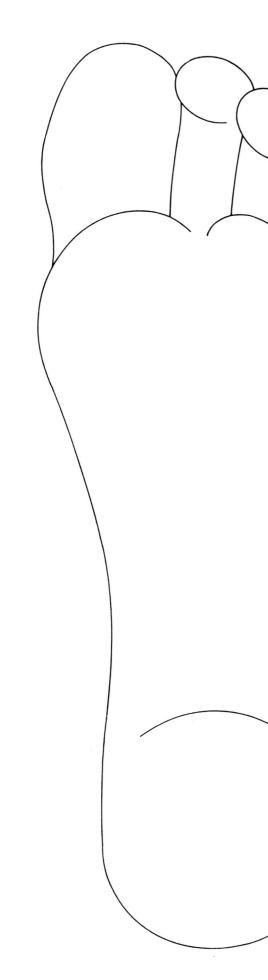

2 Tr
ba
sp
m
to

5 Ac
co
th

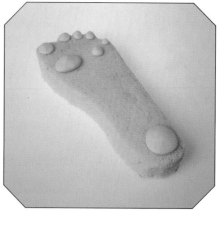

1 Using the templates as a guide, cut out two opposite feet from the sponge. Mould and fix sugarpaste domes as shown.

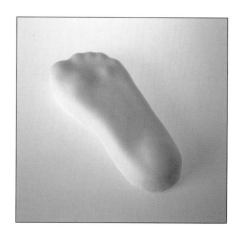

2 Cover the cakes with sugarpaste.

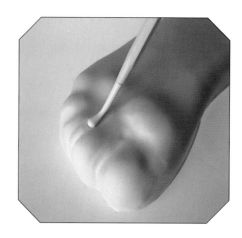

3 Using modelling tools, shape the toes and heels. Fix to cake card cut to shape then to the board. Pipe inscription of choice with royal icing (No.1).

QUILLING

Quilling creates intricate and exciting shapes from simple strips of modelling paste.

Roll the modelling paste to a thin sheet 6mm (¼in) and then cleanly cut even sized strips using a ruler and a sharp knife. Cover the unused portion with clingfilm and a damp cloth to keep it pliable. It is essential to use the template as a guide.

With the end of a paint brush, cocktail stick or a piece of dowelling, carefully roll the strip into the required shape. Fix ends with cooled boiled water or egg white, and leave to dry. Fix to cake-top with cooled boiled water or egg white.

The template design can be scratched onto the cake-top, which must be dry, as a guide.

Allow yourself plenty of time when quilling. It is a time consuming technique but the finish is well worth the effort.

INGR

20.5c
900g
115g
Asso

1 Coat the cake and board with royal icing, using a patterned scraper for the cake-side. Leave until dry. Cut lengths of modelling paste 6mm (¼in) wide. Roll over the handle of a paint brush or dowel.

2 Following the template as a guide cut and roll the strips to all the pattern shapes required. Leave until dry.

INGREDIENTS

20.5cm heart shaped cake (8in)
900g almond paste (2lb)
900g royal icing (2lb)
450g modelling paste (8oz)
Assorted food colours

EQUIPMENT and DECORATIONS

28cm heart shaped cake board (11in)
Patterned scraper
Fine paint brush or dowel
Piping tubes No.1, 2 and 3
Board edge ribbon

See: Piping shapes

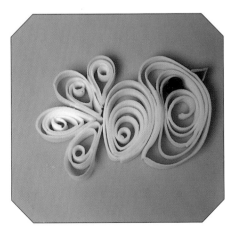

3 When the royal icing is dry, lightly transfer the design to the cake-top, then start to fix the pieces together.

4 Complete fixing the pieces to the cake-top, as shown.

5 Pipe bulbs around the cake-top edge and base (No.3). When dry, pipe a line over the bulbs (No.2) then a rope line around the board. Overpipe the No.2 line (No.1).

RIBBON LOOPS and BOWS

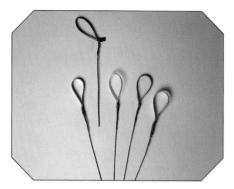

1 To make single wired ribbon loops, fold ribbon once and cut to size required. Twist wire around the ends, then tape over with floral tape.

2 To make doubled wired ribbon loops, fold ribbon twice and cut to size required. Twist wire around the ends, then tape over with floral tape.

3 To make triple wired ribbon loops, fold ribbon three times and cut to size required. Twist wire around the ends, then tape over with floral tape.

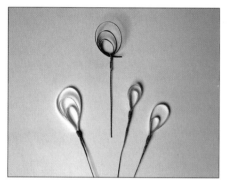

4 To make various wire ribbon loops, loop the ribbon as many times as required. Place the wire through the centre, then twist the wire around the ribbon to secure. Tape over with floral tape.

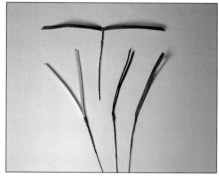

5 To make wired ribbon strands, twist wire around the centre of the ribbon length required. Tape together with floral tape.

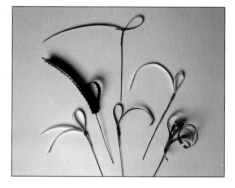

6 To make wired ribbon loops and strands, twist wire around the end of the loop leaving a length of ribbon for the strand. Tape together with floral tape.

7 To make wired multi-ribbon loops, twist wire around the centre of looped ribbon. Tape together with floral tape.

8 To make a bow, fold the ribbon over as shown to form the first loop.

9 Take the ribbon over the top and to the left.

Ribbon loops and bows can add interest to any cake. They are a vital ingredient of flower sprays and posies, but can be placed as a decorative item in their own right.

A wide variety of ribbons is available in every colour. It is usually possible to match or tone in a ribbon exactly, or contrasting colours can be used. The most usual ribbon for bows and loops is a double-faced polyester with woven edges. It has an attractive sheen and does not fray.

When choosing a ribbon, the texture and width of the ribbon will be important. A ribbon will be important. A ribbon should hold its shape and weight when folded over. Satin finished ribbons hold their shape well, and a narrow velvet finished ribbon can complement delicate flowers but care should be taken not to choose too wide a or heavy a ribbon which will overpower

small items. However, a heavier ribbon used on its own can create an impact. Florists ribbon makes interesting, curled designs which are ideal for use with flowers.

The valentine cake on page 192 illustrates how a fine synthetic ribbon can enhance a delicate arrangement of flowers, whilst the Highland wedding cake on page 198 is dramatically highlighted by the use of a darker, heavier ribbon on the cake-corners.

When working with tiered cakes, the ribbon width, and the size of loops and bows, may need to be scaled down to keep the proportions pleasing to the eye.

Floral tape and wire is used to create 'stems' for the bows and loops but wires should never be inserted into the cake. Use a small ball of sugarpaste to attach where necessary.

10 Fold and twist the ribbon half a turn, then take under and to the top right to form the knot.

11 Fold the ribbon over, then return under to form a second loop.

12 Push the loop through the knot.

13 Adjust the loops to the size of bow required, then pull tight. Trim the ends to shape shown.

1 Cover the cakes and boards with sugarpaste. When dry, transfer the designs onto the cake-sides and pipe the pattern with royal icing (No.1).

2 Pipe the dots shown, following the heart shapes (No.2).

3 Cut out and fix sugarpaste bells to the middle tier, then decorate with ribbon and ribbon bows.

4 Cut out and fix sugarpaste bells to the bottom tier, then decorate with ribbon and ribbon bows.

5 Make and fix modelling paste bells to the bottom tier and decorate with ribbon loops.

6 Fix ribbons to the top tier and then decorate with a floral spray of choice.

Small bell shaped cake
15cm round cake (6in)
20.5 x 30.5cm oblong shaped
 cake (8 x 12in)
2.5k almond paste (5lb)
3k sugarpaste (6lb)
340g royal icing (12oz)
60g modelling paste (2oz)
Lilac food colour

15cm round cake board (6in)
20.5cm round cake board (8in)
25.5 x 40.5cm oblong cake board
 (10 x 16in)
Piping tubes No.1 and 2
Narrow ribbon
Bell shaped mould
Floral sprays
Board edge ribbon

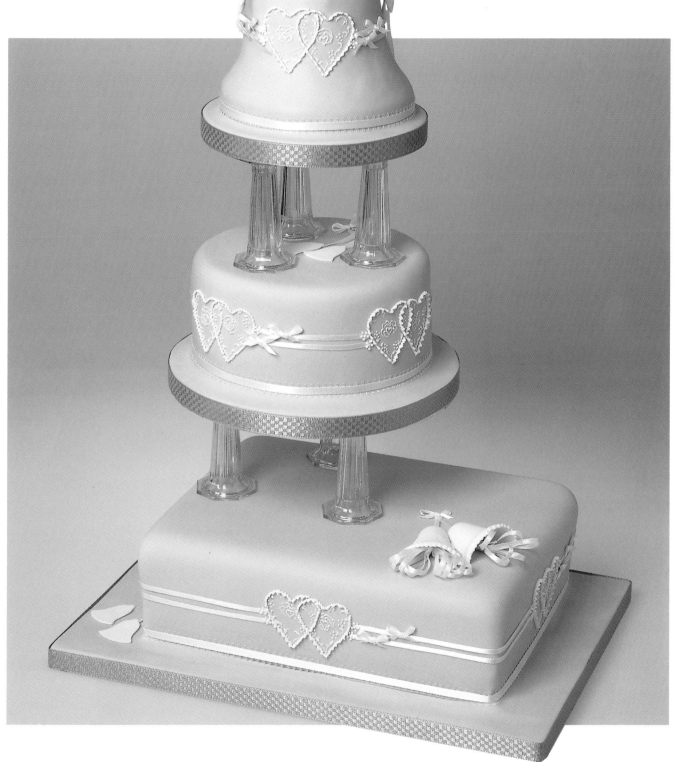

ROYAL ICED CAKES

The beautifully smooth finish to royal iced cakes makes this the traditional medium for wedding cakes that require a formal, piped design. Therefore, it is essential that great care is taken when making the icing and coating the cake as the smallest lump will mar the smoothness. All items used in the preparation should be scrupulously clean and the icing properly made. Bowls should be kept scraped down and covered with a damp cloth to prevent drying out. The bulk of the icing should be kept in a sealed container to prevent contamination. Non-ferrous tools should always be used for royal icing.

As royal icing is a form of meringue, it must be well beaten or otherwise it creates a heavy icing that is dificult to handle and sets too hard. On the other hand, over-beating the icing causes it to be too fluffy. Well made royal icing has a glossy appearance and light texture. If underbeaten, it will be slightly creamy and should be beaten further. If beaten too much, it will be grainy and heavy. A very small amount of blue colour can be incorporated into icing to improve the whiteness but this should never be added to icing which is to be coloured. The easiest way to colour icing is to add a few drops of liquid food colouring on the end of a cocktail stick. Sufficient icing to complete the work must always be made.

The consistency of the royal icing depends on the type of work involved and some icing can be made twenty fours hours in advance, whereas other techniques need freshly made icing. If stored in a refigerator, the icing must be kept in a closed container. The icing must be returned to room temperature before working.

After the cake has been decorated, it should be stored in a cardboard box, which enables the cake to breathe and air to circulate keeping it dry.

ROYAL ICING

ALBUMEN SOLUTION

INGREDIENTS

15g pure albumen powder (½oz)
85g cold water (3oz)

ROYAL ICING

INGREDIENTS

100g fresh egg whites or
albumen solution (3½oz)
450g icing sugar, sifted (1lb)

If using fresh egg whites,
separate 24 hours before use.

FOR SOFT CUTTING ROYAL ICING

For every 450g (1lb) ready-made
royal icing beat in the following
amounts of glycerin:

1tsp for bottom tier of three
tiered cake.
2tsp for middle tiers.
3tsp for top tiers, single tiers
and general piping.

**DO NOT ADD GLYCERIN WHEN MAKING
RUNOUTS, FIGURE PIPING, PIPED FLOWERS
AND LEAVES OR FINE LINE WORK.**

1 **For albumen solution:** Pour the water into a bowl, then stir and sprinkle in the albumen powder. Whisk slowly to half-blend in. The solution will go lumpy. Leave for 1 hour, stirring occasionally.

2 Pour the solution through a fine sieve or muslin. It is now ready for use. Store in a sealed container and keep in a cool place until required.

1 **For making royal icing:** Pour the egg whites or albumen solution into a bowl. Slowly mix in half the icing sugar until dissolved.

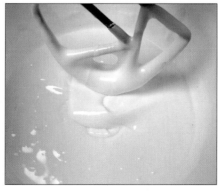

2 Then slowly mix in the remaining sugar. Run a spatula around the inside of the bowl to ensure all the ingredients are blended together.

3 Thoroughly beat mixture until light and fluffy. Peaks should be formed when the spoon or beater is lifted. Clean down inside then cover with a damp cloth until required.

RUNOUTS

Royal icing runouts can be used to create elegant collars or to produce original cake decorations.

A soft royal icing without glycerin is required for the outline and a runnier consistency for the flood-in work. An easy test for the flood-in icing is to thin down a small quantity of royal icing and then draw a sharp knife across the top. The line should close up on a count of 7 in warm weather and 10 in cold conditions. The icing should be covered with a damp cloth and allowed to stand overnight to prevent bubbles spoiling the work. Before filling the bag, tap the container hard to remove any bubbles.

The ideal surface for runout work is a glazed tile or a sheet of thick glass with waxed or non-stick paper on top. If more than one runout is required these should be made at the time to ensure a uniform finish. Dry runouts should be carefully removed from the waxed or non-stick paper and stored in a box between layers of waxed or non-stick paper until required.

Runout collars are made using the same techniques but must be carefully sized to fit the diameter of the cake. It is worth time getting the template exactly right as this can be used over and over again.

1 Make royal icing 24 hours before use. Colour sufficient icing to complete the runout as it is very difficult to match the colour later.

2 Keep a little icing aside for the outlines. Add a few drops of water to the remaining icing and stir slowly to avoid adding too much air.

3 Mix enough water into the icing to bring to a soft, but not too runny, consistency.

4 Draw the template required onto paper and secure to a flat tile or surface.

5 Place non-stick paper over the template and secure at the corners.

6 Using the unsoftened royal icing, pipe the outline following the template line (No.1).

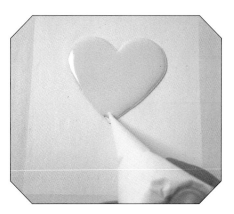

7 Fill a small piping bag with the softened royal icing and cut off the tip to make a small hole.

8 Start to fill-in the heart shape working from the top and side-to-side. Do not allow the icing to crust.

9 Flood-in the heart until the required thickness is achieved. Leave for 24 hours in a warm place or until dry.

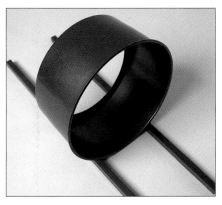

10 If the heart runout is to be fixed to the cake-side, use the cake tin on its side as shown.

11 Immediately after the heart has been flooded-in, gently raise off the template and hold between the hands as shown.

12 Place onto the cake tin and secure with a little royal icing at each corner. Leave until dry.

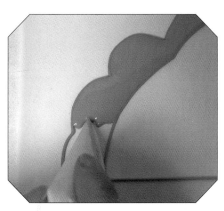

13 When making a large runout flood-in part of one side as shown.

14 Then flood-in part of the opposite side, filling the runout from side-to-side until complete.

15 Cut a small cross in the centre to avoid the non-stick paper creasing as the royal icing dries.

RUNOUTS: CONFIRMATION

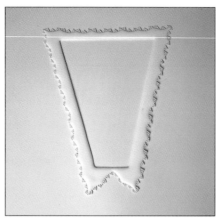

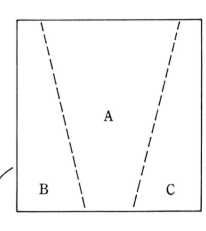

1 Using the templates as a guide, cut the cake and fix the pieces together to form the shape shown. Cover with almond paste, then coat with royal icing. Leave until dry. Coat the board with royal icing. When dry, place the cake onto the coated board. Using the template as a guide, mark the pattern around the cake-base. Pipe a line with royal icing (No.1) then fill-in the pattern with softened royal icing. Leave until dry.

2 Outline (No.1) and flood-in, onto non-stick paper, the cake-top collar as shown. Leave until dry. Pipe dots around the runout (No.1). Leave until dry.

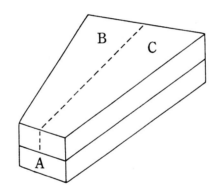

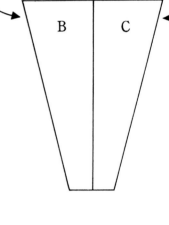

3 Pipe-in the rose onto non-stick paper and leave until dry. 4 required.

4 When dry, pipe dots around the cake-base run out (No.1) then pipe shells around the cake-base (No.2). When dry, remove the cake-top runout from the paper.

5 Pipe a line on the cake-top edge (No.2), then immediately fix the cake-top run out in position. Fix the roses to the cake-sides. Pipe inscription of choice (No.1) and decorate as required.

20.5cm madeira cake (8in)
450g almond paste (1lb)
900g royal icing (2lb)
Cream, peach and green food
 colours

23 x 30cm oblong cake board (9 x 12in)
Non-stick paper
Piping tubes No.1 and 2

Sugar doves and blossoms
Floral spray
Board edge ribbon

15cm round cake (6in)
25.5cm round cake (10in)
2k almond paste (4lb)
2k royal icing (4lb)
Blue food colour

23cm round cake board (9in)
33cm round cake board (13in)
Piping tubes No.1, 2, 3 and 43
Decorations of choice
Board edge ribbon

See: Extension work
Piping shapes

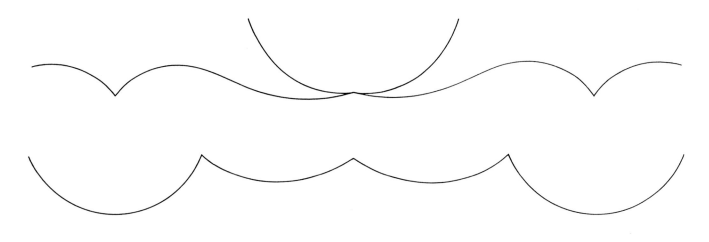

Using the templates as a guide, scratch the lines onto the cake and then follow with the piping.

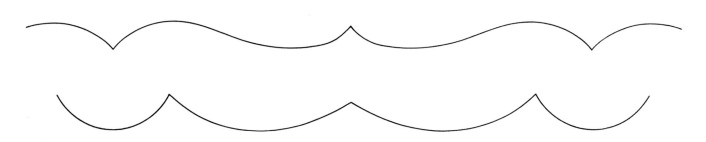

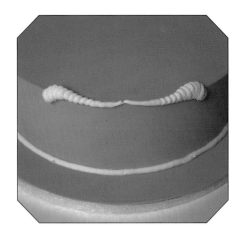

1 Coat the cakes and boards with royal icing. When dry, pipe a line around the cake-base (No.43). Mark the cake-top edge into 12 divisions then pipe 'S' scrolls as shown (No.43).

2 Continue piping the scrolls around the cake-top edge and then around the cake-base.

3 Using the template as a guide, pipe 'C' scrolls onto the cake-top as shown.

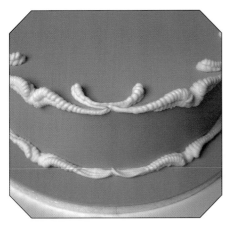

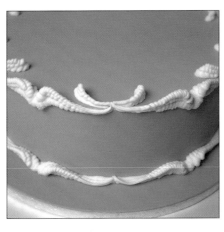

4 Overpipe all the cake-top and cake-base scrolls (No.3).

5 Overpipe all the cake-top and cake-base scrolls (No.2).

6 Support the cake on a solid base to tilt approximately 45°, then pipe the lines shown around the cake side (No.2).

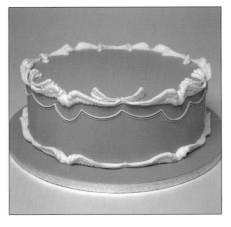

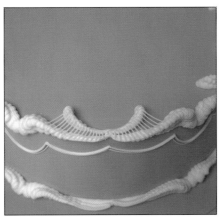

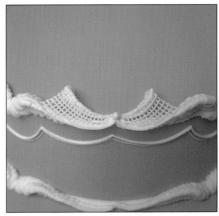

7 Pipe a line below the No.2 line and then against the No.2 line (No.1).

8 Pipe lines across the scrolls as shown (No.1). Leave until dry.

9 When dry, pipe the additional lines shown to form lattice (No.1). Overpipe the scrolls, to hide the lattice edges, then pipe a dot at the centre (No.1).

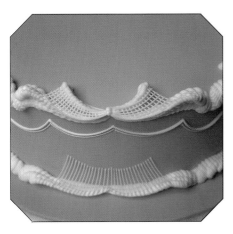

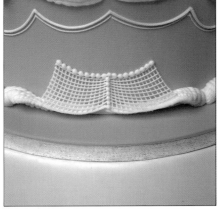

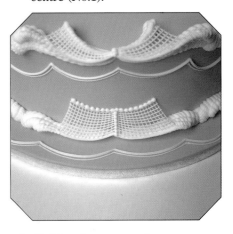

10 Pipe the suspended lines around the cake-side (No.1) piping from the cake to the scroll. Leave until dry.

11 Pipe across the lines to form the lattice, overpipe the scrolls and then pipe shells as shown (No.1.)

12 Pipe the pattern shown onto the cake board (No.2). Pipe a line beside the No.2 line and then overpipe the No.2 line (No.1). Fix decorations of choice and ribbon around the cake board edge.

SILHOUETTES

A silhouette can either be painted directly onto a royal iced or sugarpaste covered cake, or onto a sugarpaste plaque. It looks extremely dramatic when worked in black and white, but a more subtle effect can be created in light and dark shades of the same colour.

The technique is a simple one of painting in the design with diluted food colour, adding additional coats until the required depth of colour is achieved. The cake can be designed with a suitable 'frame' or a decorative border added around a plaque.

Portraits of favourite pets or animals are always appreciated, and an unusual birthday or wedding anniversary present would be to create a plaque from a photograph. To do this, enlarge the photograph on a photocopier and then trace onto the cake or plaque. Alternatively, throw a shadow onto a piece of white paper and trace around it. Reduce on a photocopier and transfer to the cake.

Birthday cards, magazine pictures and Japanese designs are ideal for the silhouette treatment. Teenagers are always delighted to receive a silhouette of their favourite pop or sports star, especially if this is on a plaque that can be kept as a souvenir.

INGREDIENTS

20.5cm square cake (8in)
900g almond paste (2lb)
1.25k sugarpaste (2½lb)
115g royal icing (4oz)
Assorted food colours

EQUIPMENT and DECORATIONS

28cm square cake board (11in)
Fine paint brush
Piping tube No.1
Ivy leaf cutter
Narrow ribbon
Board edge ribbon

1 Cover the cake and board with sugarpaste. Leave until dry. Using the template as a guide, transfer the design shown onto the cake-top. Brush-in with black food colour.

2 Trace designs onto the cake-side and brush with black food colour. Pipe the ground with royal icing. Fix narrow ribbon around the cake-base.

3 Cut out sugarpaste ivy leaves. Pipe irregular lines with royal icing (No.1) around the cake-base and corners, then fix the leaves. Pipe inscription of choice (No.1).

SMOCKING

Smocking is a traditional technique used to decorate clothes. It makes an attractive decoration for cakes and many ideas can be found in needlecraft books, especially older editions.

The easiest paste to use is sugarpaste to which a little gum tragacanth has been added, or flower paste which holds the delicate shape well.

The paste has to be indented to resemble gathered material. The quickest way to do this is to use a ruler, or ribbed roller, and tweezers as shown. (If a rounded, ribbed effect is required, the paste can be placed with cocktail sticks alternately under and over the paste but this is extremely time consuming and requires twice the amount of paste). The 'material' is then embroidered with royal icing to resemble smocking stitches.

INGREDIENTS

25.5cm petal shaped cake (10in)
1.5k almond paste (3lb)
1.75k sugarpaste (3½lb)
225g flower paste (8oz)
225g royal icing (8oz)
Peach food colour

EQUIPMENT and DECORATIONS

33cm round cake board (13in)
Rule or ribbed roller
Tweezers
Miniature heart cutter

Piping tube No.1
Extended lace cutter
Miniature horseshoes
Board edge ribbon

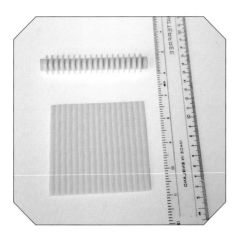

1 Roll out and cut a square of sugarpaste. Using a rule, or ribbed roller, mark the sugarpaste in rows as shown.

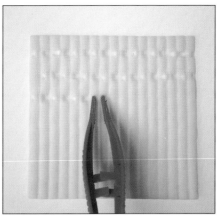

2 With a pair of tweezers squeeze the lines together in parallel rows.

3 Pipe a short line in each indent with royal icing (No.1).

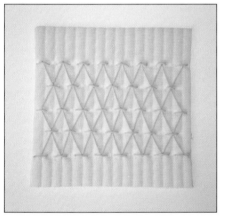

4 Pipe diagonal lines as shown to create the smocking effect.

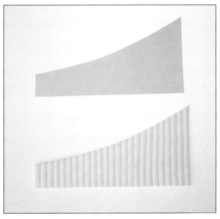

5 Cut out a paper template to fit the cake-side shape required, then follow steps 1 to 2 and fix to the cake-side.

6 Follow steps 3 to 4 as shown.

7 Roll out a thin sheet of sugarpaste and cut to cake shape. Cut out small hearts then fix the sugarpaste to the cake-top. Cut out and fix flower paste lace to the cake-side.

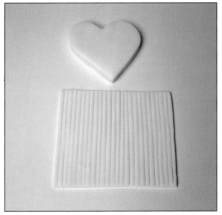

8 Cut out a large sugarpaste heart. Cut out a thin sheet of sugarpaste, mark as in step 1 and fix to the heart.

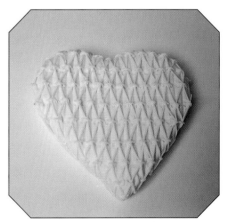

9 Follow steps 2 to 4 to decorate the heart as shown. Fix to the cake-top with cut-out sugarpaste lace.

SUGARPASTE

Sugarpaste is a beautifully silky, delicate and smooth covering that has a sweet taste. Its flowing lines need the minimum of decoration to create a stunning cake. It is the ideal medium for beginners to work in as extremely elegant designs can be created with the minimum of experience and few specialist tools.

Sugarpaste can be coloured and flavoured easily. Edible paste food colouring should be used. Dip a cocktail stick into the colour and add a very small amount at a time to the paste. Knead well until the colour is thoroughly blended. If a marbled effect is required, mix until streaky and then roll out. If graduated colouring is required, mix the darkest shade first then add more white sugarpaste to create paler shades. Once coloured, the sugarpaste should be protected from strong light and stored in a sealed container. It must not be kept in a refrigerator. The completed cake should be stored in a cardboard box and kept at 18°C (65°F).

Sugarpaste for covering should be made at least 24 hours before use and kept in an airtight container. If the paste is found to be too dry too roll out, add a little white fat to the mixture. If the paste is too sticky, a little cornflour or icing sugar can be added. Sugarpaste should be rolled out on an icing sugar dusted surface.

When applying sugarpaste, great care should be taken not to trap any air under the paste. The paste should be smoothed with the flat of the hand and then polished with a smoother or the palm of the hand. The cake should be left until a crust has formed on the surface unless it is to be crimped, embossed etc.

INGREDIENTS

2tbsp cold water	2tsp glycerin
1½ level tsp powdered gelatine	450g icing sugar, sifted (1lb)
1½tbsp liquid glucose	

1 Pour the water into a saucepan and sprinkle on the powdered gelatine. Dissolve over low heat. Stir in the glucose and glycerin then remove from the heat.

2 Gradually add and stir in the icing sugar with a spoon, to avoid making a lumpy mixture. When unable to stir anymore icing sugar into mixture, turn out onto table.

3 Mix in the remaining icing sugar using fingers then knead until a pliable smooth paste is formed. Store in a sealed container until required.

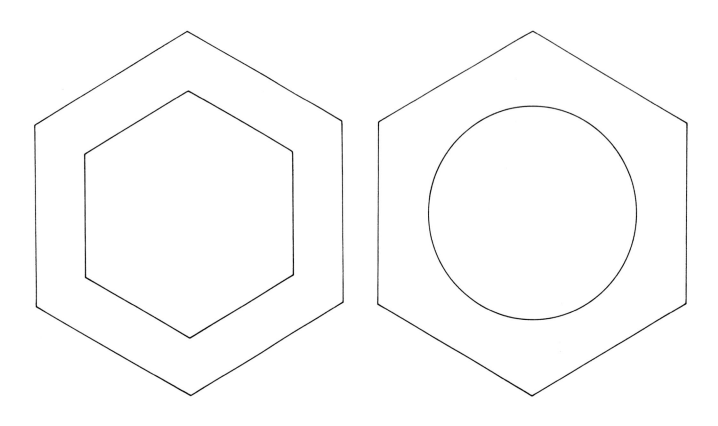

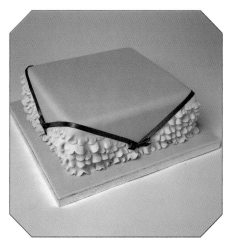

1 Cover the cakes and boards with sugarpaste. Mark from each top corner to the middle of the cake-base. Roll out, cut and frill sugarpaste band and fix to the cake-side as shown.

2 Continue making and fixing frills to form the triangular shape, following the marked line.

3 Fix narrow ribbon along the edges then make and fix ribbon bows.

INGREDIENTS

15cm square cake (6in)
20.5cm square cake (8in)
2k almond paste (4lb)
2.5k sugarpaste (5lb)
225g modelling paste (8oz)
115g royal icing (4oz)
Brown food colour

EQUIPMENT and DECORATIONS

23cm square cake board (9in)
28cm square cake board (11in)
Frill cutter
Cocktail stick
Lace cutter
Miniature heart cutter
Small bell mould
Piping tube No.1

Narrow ribbons
Domed mould
2 Sugar birds
Flowers and leaves
Board edge ribbon

See: Flowers
Frills

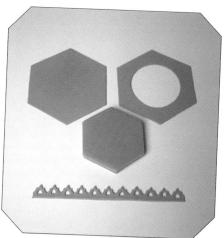

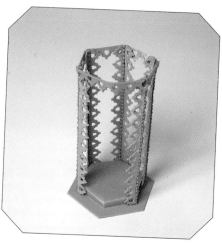

4 With modelling paste, cut out the hexagonal pieces shown, using the templates as a guide. Cut lengths of modelling paste using a lace cutter. 10 required plus short pieces for the top and base. Leave to dry.

5 Place a thin piece of modelling paste over a domed mould, slightly larger than the cut-out top hexagonal. Cut out the hearts. Make 2 bells, using a bell mould. Leave to dry.

6 When dry, fix the base pieces together then assemble the frame. Fix the sides together with piped shells, using royal icing (No.1).

1 Layer the c
edge of the
shape. The
boards with

4 Pipe cont
cake-top c
(No.2). Le

7 When dry, fix the top hexagonal and dome. Pipe the shells shown (No.1).

8 Fix the bells, using taped wire, and then the birds to the top.

9 Fix a cluster of flowers onto the cake-top centre and to each corner. Fix the top ornament and decorate with flowers.

Round Templates

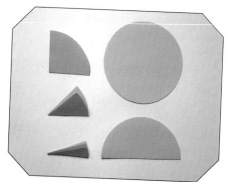

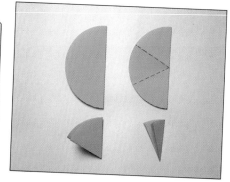

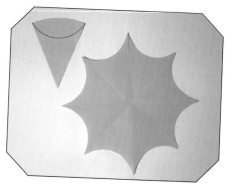

1 To form 2, 4, 8 or 16 sections.
Cut paper to fit cake-top (1).
Fold (1) = (2) – 2 sections
Fold (2) = (3) – 4 sections
Fold (3) = (4) – 8 sections
Fold (4) = (5) – 16 sections

2 To form 2, 6 or 12 sections.
Cut paper to fit cake-top.
Fold = (1) – 2 sections
Mark (1) into 3 equal sections = (2).
Fold (2) = (3) – 6 sections
Fold (3) = (4) – 12 sections

3 = 8 sections.
Follow instructions in 'A' to make 8 sections. Mark the curve shown and cut. Unfold and place centrally on cake top.

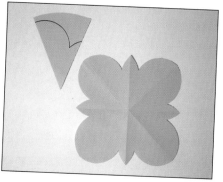

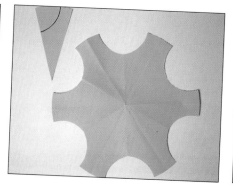

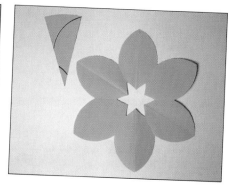

4 = 8 sections.
Follow instructions in 'A' to make 8 sections. Mark the curves shown and cut. Unfold and place centrally on cake-top.

5 = 12 sections.
Follow instructions in 'B' to make 12 sections. Mark the curve shown and cut. Unfold and place centrally on cake-top.

6 = 12 sections.
Follow instructions in 'B' to make 12 sections. Mark the curves shown and cut. Unfold and place centrally on cake-top.

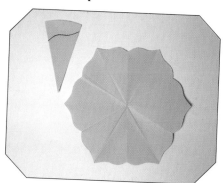

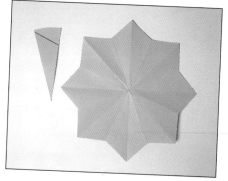

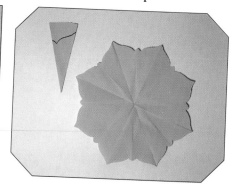

7 = 12 sections.
Follow instructions in 'B' to make 12 sections. Mark the curves shown and cut. Unfold and place centrally on cake-top.

8 = 16 sections.
Follow instructions in 'A' to make 16 sections. Mark the line shown and cut. Unfold and place centrally on cake-top.

9 = 16 sections.
Follow instructions in 'A' to make 16 sections. Mark the curve shown and cut. Unfold and place centrally on cake-top.

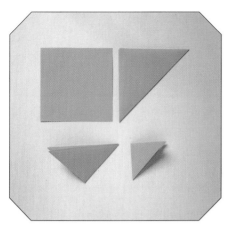

10 **Square Templates**
Cut paper to fit cake-top.
Fold (1) diagonally = (2)
Fold (2) in half = (3)
Fold (3) in half = (4)

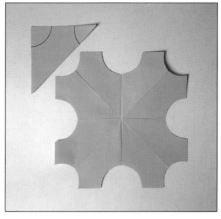

11 Follow whole sequence in A.
Mark the curve shown and cut.
Unfold and place centrally on cake-top.

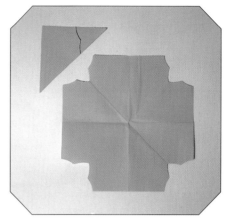

12 Follow whole sequence in A.
Mark the curve shown and cut.
Unfold and place centrally on cake-top.

13 Follow whole sequence in A.
Mark the curve shown and cut.
Unfold and place centrally on cake-top.

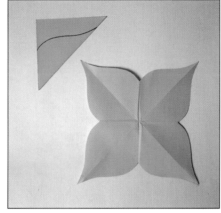

14 Follow whole sequence in A.
Mark the curve shown and cut.
Unfold and place centrally on cake-top.

15 Follow whole sequence in A.
Mark the curve shown and cut.
Unfold and place centrally on cake-top.

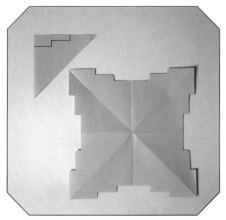

16 Follow whole sequence in A.
Mark the line shown and cut.
Unfold and place centrally on cake-top.

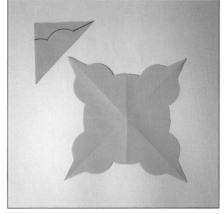

17 Follow whole sequence in A.
Mark the lines shown and cut.
Unfold and place centrally on cake-top.

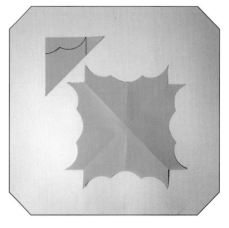

18 Follow whole sequence in A.
Mark the curves shown and cut.
Unfold and place centrally on cake-top.

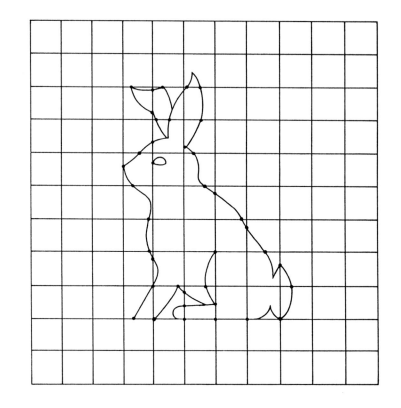

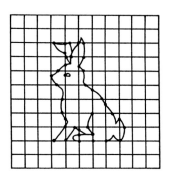

Explanatory note:

Templates can be increased or decreased in size to compliment the size of cake being decorated. This can be achieved by using the following instructions.

Instructions:

1 Draw the template from the book onto greaseproof paper. Place onto the template graph and draw in the squares.

2 Count the number of squares used on the template.

3 Measure the actual size of the template required and draw the same number of squares onto a clean piece of paper to that size required.

4 Where the template crosses the lines on the original drawing mark a dot onto the new squares.

5 Join the dots together to form the final template required.

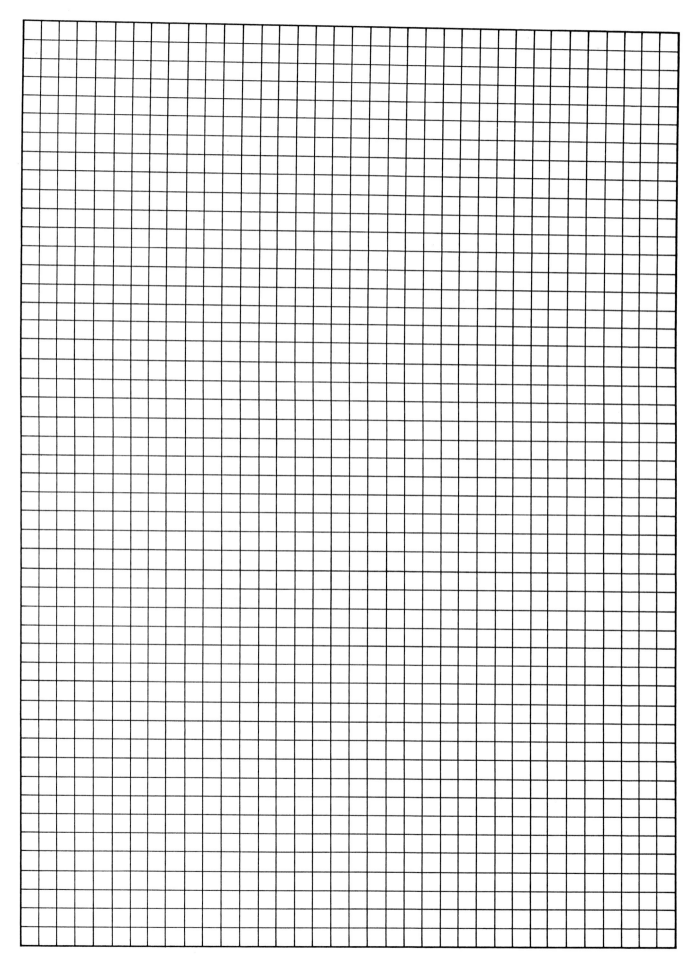

THREE-D

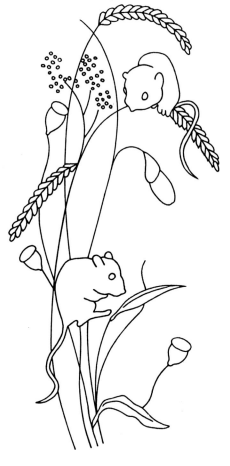

1 Cover the cake and board with sugarpaste. Leave until dry. Pipe shells around the cake-base (No.2). Trace the template onto the cake-top. Pipe-in the picture with royal icing. When dry paint as required.

2 Make a selection of wired flowers and foliage with flower paste.

3 Fix flowers to the picture with a small piece of sugarpaste, as shown. Do not push the wires into the cake.

4 Fix bunches of flowers and foliage around the cake-base. Pipe inscription of choice (No.1).

20.5cm petal shaped cake (8in)
680g almond paste (1½lb)
680g sugarpaste (1½lb)
115g flower paste (4oz)
115g royal icing (4oz)
Assorted food colours

28cm round cake board (11in)
Piping tubes No.1 and 2
Floral wire and tape
Flower cutters
Fine paint brush
Board edge ribbon

TRANSFERRING DESIGNS

All the cakes in this book are accompanied by templates where necessary. However, it is easy to find new inspiration in children's story books or birthday or christmas cards, and in specialist pattern books.

If the design is not exactly the right size, it can quickly be increased or decreased on an enlarging photocopier. A design which is in proportion to the cake-top size looks harmonious, but extra impact can be added by increasing the size.

When preparing designs for collars, trace the design onto tracing paper and then glue onto a cut-out card collar. Place on the cake-top, check fit and adjust if necessary.

When using card templates for runouts and brushed embroidery, trace or draw the design onto a piece of card. Cut out all the sections. Place the sections on the cake-top and pipe round each piece (No.1). Carefully remove each piece of card once the icing is dry.

When tracing onto the cake-top, trace the template onto greaseproof paper using a food approved pen. Retrace the lines on the back of the tracing paper. Turn the paper over and place on the cake-top. Trace again using a food approved pen. Designs can also be scratched or pricked onto the cake top with a scriber or sharp tool, as shown.

A very delicate design can be created by piping royal icing onto a clear sheet, using a template if necessary, and then pressing the dried icing onto a sugarpaste covered cake. The embossing must be done while the sugarpaste is soft.

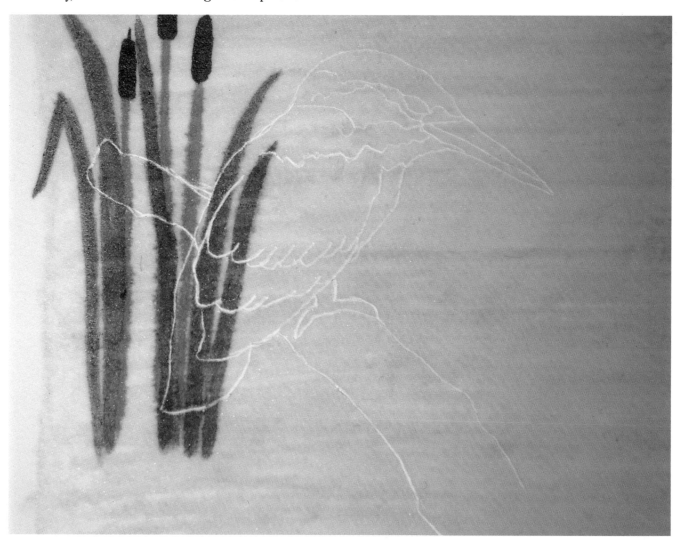

25.5cm square cake (10in)
1.5k almond paste (3lb)
1.75k royal icing (3½lb)
Assorted food colours

35.5cm square cake board (14in)
Scriber
Fine paint brushes
Non-stick paper

Piping tubes No.1, 2, 3 and 44
Board edge ribbon

See: Piping figures
Piping shapes

1 Coat the cake and board with royal icing. When dry, paint the water and bulrushes onto the cake-top, using the template as a guide. Leave to dry.

2 Scratch the outlines of the Kingfisher and log with a scriber.

3 Pipe-in the parts of the Kingfisher and log, with royal icing.

4 Pipe-in the further parts shown.

5 Pipe-in the further parts shown then paint in the eye.

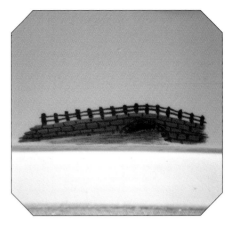

6 Pipe-in the lilies onto non-stick paper and fix when dry, or pipe directly onto the cake-top. Brush the ripples as shown.

7 Using the template as a guide, brush the picture shown onto opposite cake-sides.

8 Repeat step 7 with the design shown for the remaining sides.

9 Pipe graduated dots to form pebbles at the cake-base centres (No.2). Pipe graduated shells around the cake-base as shown (No.44). Pipe a line over the shells (No.2).

10 Pipe a continuous rope line over the No.2 line (No.2).

11 Pipe scrolls on the cake-top edges shown (No.44).

12 Pipe shells on the remaining cake-top edges (No.3).

13 Overpipe the scrolls (No.3). Then overpipe the No.3 scroll (No.2).

14 Lightly stipple around the board edge to form ground effect. Pipe inscription of choice (No.1) then pipe the tracery as shown, on the main picture.

TULLE

This delicate medium produces exquisite designs. Only the finest tulle is suitable for shaped creations as a wide mesh would allow the piped royal icing to fall through. Bridal veiling, available from dressmaking, shops is ideal. As this only comes in white or cream, the tulle can be soaked in diluted food colouring before use.

When necessary, the tulle can be pinned to a cake board to keep it taut. When pinning, the pin must go through a hole and not where a line will be piped. The tulle should be laid on non-stick paper on a flat or curved surface according to the shape required. A template can be placed underneath. The shape is then piped using royal icing without glycerin and a No.1 tube. Shapes such as butterflies may need supporting with foam until dry.

Tulle is ideal for creating frills. A strip two and a half times the circumference of the cake should be gathered up to fit using a running stitch. The frill is then anchored in place using royal icing piped with a No.1 tube, and the join covered with ribbon. The bottom of a frill can be scalloped by folding the frill, concertina style, to about 5cm (2in) and cutting one or two curves in the bottom edge. delicate piping looks extremely attractive on a frill, but it can be left plain if desired.

If clothes or three dimensional items such as churches, bells or flowers, are being created, the tulle should be sewn or shaped before piping. Work on the back first, allowing the item to dry before turning over and working on the front.

Tulle can also be worked for side decorations and extension work. The individual pieces should be cut out using a template and carefully attached to the cake with pins before piping a scalloped line over the join. The line should touch both the cake and the tulle. Once the join is dry, the tulle can be piped in to create a decorative border. Remove the pins when dry.

To stiffen tulle:

Dissolve 85g (3oz) icing sugar in 145g (5oz) water. Bring to the boil and simmer for 10 minutes. Cool and bottle. Store in a refrigerator. Soak tulle in the mixture, drain off excess liquid and remove surplus using kitchen paper. Fasten over mould if required (surplus tulle can be held with an elastic band and trimmed before use). Pipe while still damp. Allow to dry before use.

20.5cm round cake (8in)
680g almond paste (1½lb)
900g sugarpaste (2lb)
225g royal icing (8oz)
Assorted food colours

28cm round cake board (11in)
Tulle
Glass headed pins
Piping tubes No.1 and 2
Non-stick paper

Narrow ribbon
Miniature blossoms
Board edge ribbon

See: Lace

1 Cover the cake and board with sugarpaste. Using the template as a guide cut out a piece of tulle and then cut out a sugarpaste sole.

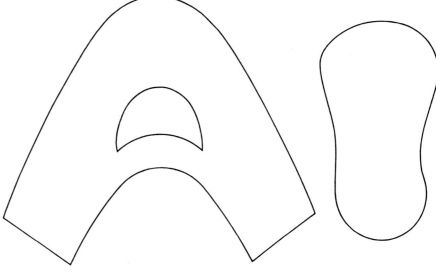

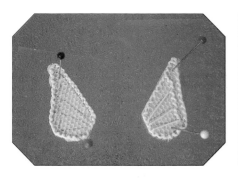

2 Pipe a line with royal icing (No.1) around the edge of the sole and fix the tulle in position, using the pins to secure whilst drying. 2 required.

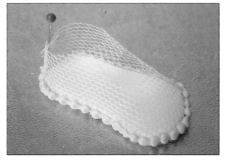

3 When dry, pipe shells around the edge of the shoes (No.2). Leave until dry.

4 When dry, pipe filigree over the shoes then small shells around the openings (No.1). Leave until dry.

5 Cut out tulle butterfly wings, pin to non-stick paper then pipe the scalloped lines shown (No.1). 2 pairs required. Leave until dry.

6 When dry, pipe a butterfly body onto non-stick paper (No.1) and then fix the wings in position and support until dry.

7 Pipe 70 pieces of lace onto non-stick paper (No.1). Leave until dry. Gather tulle as shown for the floral spray. Fix the various pieces to the cake then pipe inscription of choice (No.1).

TULLE COLLAR

INGREDIENTS

EQUIPMENT and DECORATIONS

25.5cm oval cake (10in)
1.25k almond paste (2½lb)
1.75k sugarpaste (3½lb)
225g royal icing (8oz)
Pink, cream and moss green
 food colours

35.5cm oval cake board (14in)
Tulle
Piping tube No.1
Floral spray
Sugar butterfly

Narrow ribbon
Board edge ribbon

See: Flowers
 Tracery

190

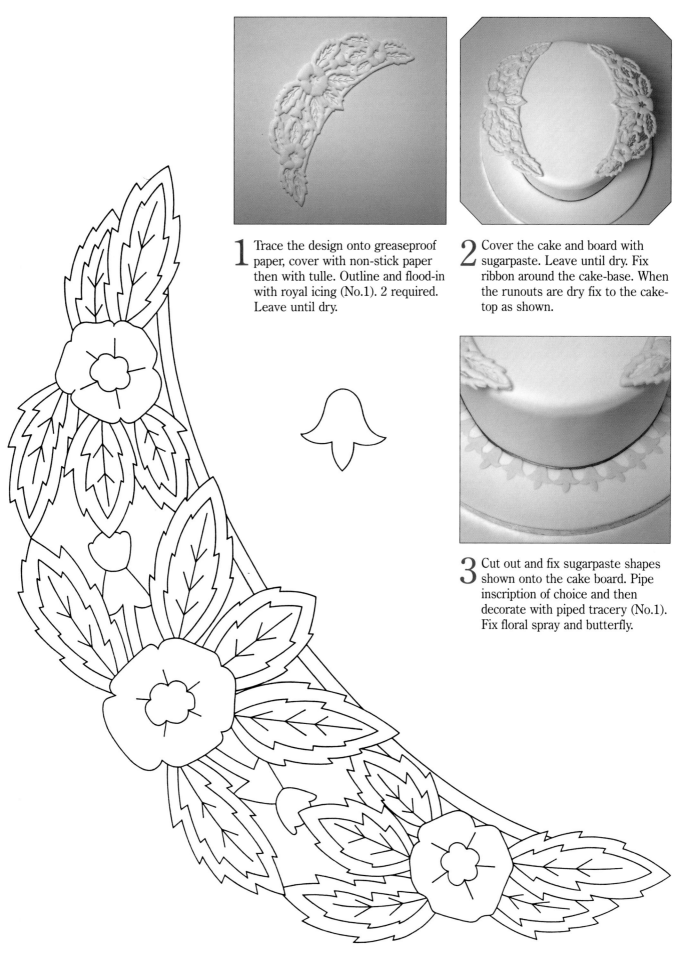

1 Trace the design onto greaseproof paper, cover with non-stick paper then with tulle. Outline and flood-in with royal icing (No.1). 2 required. Leave until dry.

2 Cover the cake and board with sugarpaste. Leave until dry. Fix ribbon around the cake-base. When the runouts are dry fix to the cake-top as shown.

3 Cut out and fix sugarpaste shapes shown onto the cake board. Pipe inscription of choice and then decorate with piped tracery (No.1). Fix floral spray and butterfly.

VALENTINE

INGREDIENTS

25.5cm heart shaped cake (10in)
1.5k almond paste (3lb)
1.5k sugarpaste (3lb)
450g royal icing (1lb)
Pink food colour

EQUIPMENT and DECORATIONS

35.5cm heart shaped cake board (14in)
Tulle or net
Piping tube No.1
Floral spray
Board edge ribbon

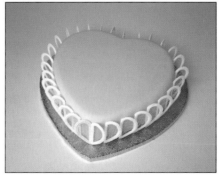

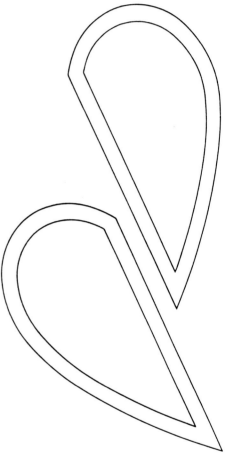

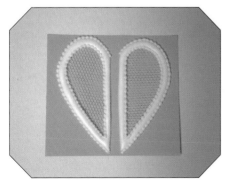

1 Cover the cake with sugarpaste. Using the template as a guide, outline and flood-in runout pieces shown onto tulle fixed to non-stick paper. 16 pairs required.

2 When the runouts are dry, fix to the cake-side as shown.

3 Pipe inscription of choice and decorate with tracery (No.1). Fix floral spray and board edge ribbon.

WEDDING CAKE

Timing

With its excellent keeping properties, fruit cake is the traditional medium for wedding cakes. Make the cake seven to eight weeks before the wedding date. The cake should then be wrapped in waxed paper and left in a cupboard for at least three weeks to mature. The almond paste covering should be completed three weeks prior to the date, and the royal icing or sugarpaste one week before hand. The sugarpaste or royal icing should be left for twenty-four hours before decorating. Sugarcraft decorations, such as sugar flowers, can be made in advance and stored in cardboard boxes until required.

Size and shape

The size and shape of the cake should be based on the number of guests. It is traditional to save the top tier for an anniversary or christening, so the bottom tiers should be large enough to serve all the guests. To calculate the approximate number of portions that may be cut from the finished cake, add up the total weight of all the cake ingredients, almond paste, sugarpaste or royal icing. Divide the total by 60g (2oz). A 30cm (12in) round cake yields approximately 100 portions, the same diameter square cake approximately 134 portions. An additional plain iced cake can be kept in reserve for extra portions if required.

The sharp lines of a royal iced cake are particularly suitable for a cake with pillars supporting the tiers. The gentler lines of a sugarpaste-covered cake are ideal for the flowing lines of modern cake stands.

Colour

Remember that icing always dries a little darker than at first appears. Cakes can be coloured to tone in with the bridal flowers, bridesmaids dresses, etc. or to provide an area of contrast. Graduated shades for different tiers can be appealing, and a deep tone can look very sophisticated with pale or white icing. Too pale a shade should be avoided as it can look washed out.

Tiers

It is traditional to have a 5cm (2in) graduation between the tiers on a royal iced cake. However, sugarpaste-covered cakes may well have a 5cm (3in) difference in diameter, with the depth of the tiers remaining the same. If a centrepiece such as a vase of flowers is to form the focal point, then a difference of only 5cm (2in) produces a more pleasing overall effect. Pillars for a royal iced cake should decrease in height, whilst the depth of pillars for a sugarpaste covered cake remains the same.

If tiering a sugarpaste covered cake, special food approved supports should be used. Dowelling can be placed inside hollow pillars to support the weight of an upper tier. The wine glasses used on page 84 make an attractive support as the wide bases support the weight.
Alternatively, small cake cards can be used beneath the pillars.

Not to Scale

6.5cm (2½in)

7.5cm (3in)

For a 20.5cm (8in) cake, pillars should be positioned 6.5cm (2½in) from the centre. For a 25.5cm (10in) cake, pillars should be positioned 7.5cm (3in) from the centre. A square cake usually has 4 pillars which can be on the diagonal or the cross, whichever suits the design best. A round cake usually has 3 pillars in a triangle, or four arranged in a circle.

TIERING A SUGARPASTE-COVERED CAKE

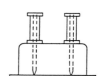

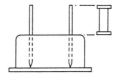

1 Push food-approved rods into the cake to the board. Cut rods to height of pillar.

2 Place the pillars over the rods.

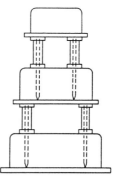

3 Assemble the cake, as required.

WEDDING CAKE

For hexagonal, octagonal or petal shaped wedding cakes use recipe for the equivalent round cake. Example, for 20.5cm (8in) heart shape use ingredients for 20.5cm (8in) round cake.

Square tin OR Round tin	12.5cm (5in) / 15cm (6in)	15cm (6in) / 18cm (7in)	18cm (7in) / 20.5cm (8in)	20.5cm (8in) / 23cm (9in)	23cm (9in) / 25.5cm (10in)	25.5cm (10in) / 28cm (11in)	28cm (11in) / 30.5cm (12in)
Sultanas	170g (6oz)	255g (9oz)	340g (12oz)	425g (15oz)	515g (18oz)	600g (21oz)	680g (24oz)
Currants	170g (6oz)	255g (9oz)	340g (12oz)	425g (15oz)	515g (18oz)	600g (21oz)	680g (24oz)
Raisins	60g (2oz)	85g (3oz)	115g (4oz)	145g (5oz)	170g (6oz)	200g (7oz)	225g (8oz)
Candied peel	30g (1oz)	30g (1oz)	60g (2oz)	85g (3oz)	115g (4oz)	145g (5oz)	200g (7oz)
Glacé cherries	60g (2oz)	60g (2oz)	85g (3oz)	115g (4oz)	170g (6oz)	225g (8oz)	285g (10oz)
Lemon rind (lemons)	½	½	1	1	1	1½	2
Rum/Brandy	1tbsp	1tbsp	1tbsp	1½tbsp	2tbsp	2½tbsp	3tbsp
Butter	115g (4oz)	170g (6oz)	225g (8oz)	285g (10oz)	340g (12oz)	400g (14oz)	450g (1lb)
Dark brown soft sugar	115g (4oz)	170g (6oz)	225g (8oz)	285g (10oz)	340g (12oz)	400g (14oz)	450g (1lb)
Eggs, size 2	1½	2½	4	4½	6	7	8
Ground almonds	30g (1oz)	60g (2oz)	85g (3oz)	85g (3oz)	115g (4oz)	145g (5oz)	200g (7oz)
Plain flour, sifted	115g (4oz)	170g (6oz)	225g (8oz)	285g (10oz)	340g (12oz)	400g (14oz)	450g (1lb)
Ground mace	small pinch	small pinch	medium pinch	medium pinch	large pinch	large pinch	large pinch
Mixed spice	¼tsp	½tsp	¾tsp	1tsp	1¼tsp	1½tsp	1¾tsp
Ground nutmeg	pinch	pinch	¼tsp	½tsp	½tsp	¾tsp	1tsp
Black treacle	½tbsp	½tbsp	1tbsp	1tbsp	1½tbsp	1½tbsp	2tbsp
Baking temperature	\multicolumn{7}{c}{140°C (275°F) or Gas Mark 1}						
Approximate baking time	2½hrs	3hrs	3½hrs	4hrs	5hrs	6hrs	7½hrs

HINTS AND TIPS

Always line the inside of the cake tin carefully to prevent a mis-shaped cake.

Add egg slowly to batter otherwise it will curdle and result in a poor texture, volume, crumb structure and keeping quality.

Beat in a little of the flour if the batter starts to curdle.

Stir the flour thoroughly into the batter before adding the fruit but be careful not to overmix as this will toughen the batter.

Flour is best added with a wooden spoon.

Batter that has been overbeaten will not support the fruit adequately, causing the fruit to sink during baking.

Always make sure that fruit is clean and is as dry as possible. Do not overwash the fruit.

The cake mixture may be left for up to 24 hours in the tin before baking.

Never bake a cake in a brand new shiny tin. (Remove the shine by placing tin in a hot oven.)

Be careful not to bake in an oven that is too hot. It will produce a cake that has a cracked, crusted top and an uncooked centre. It will also be dark in colour and have bitter tasting, burnt fruit around its crust.

An oven which is too cool produces a pale cake with uncooked fruit and a very thick crust. The cake will go dry and will not keep.

A cake that has been baked at the correct temperature yet sinks in the middle is caused by too much liquid, sugar, fat, or baking powder in the mixture.

The following may result in a cake that is too crumbly: curdled batter, overbeating the fat, sugar and eggs, undermixing the flour and fruit into the batter, insufficient sugar.

WEDDING CAKE

Fruit cake is the traditional medium for wedding cakes as it has excellent keeping properties. When making a fruit cake, timing is important, as it needs at least three weeks to mature.

BAKING TEST At the end of the recommended baking time, bring the cake forward from the oven so that it can be tested.

Insert a stainless steel skewer into the centre of the cake and slowly withdraw it. The cake has been sufficiently baked if the skewer comes out as cleanly as it went in. If the cake mixture clings to the skewer, remove the skewer and continue baking at the same temperature. Test in the same manner every 10 minutes until the skewer is clean when withdrawn from the cake.

SOAKING MIXTURE Equal quantities of glycerin mixed with rum, sherry or any spirits of your choice. The recommended amount of mixture when soaking the cake is 15ml per 450g of cake (1 full tablespoon per 1lb of cake).

STORAGE Carefully remove the cake from the tin when it is cold and then remove the greaseproof paper. Wrap the cake in waxed paper and leave in a cupboard for at least three weeks to mature.

1 Using table as a guide weigh the ingredients into separate containers. Double check the quantities then mix the prepared fruit and rum/brandy together in a bowl. Leave overnight to soak.

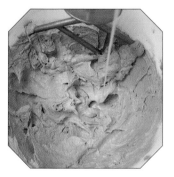

2 Grease the tin with melted butter, line with greaseproof paper then grease the paper. Beat the butter and sugar together until light and fluffy. Then thoroughly beat in the eggs, a little at a time.

3 Stir in the ground almonds, then fold in sifted flour and spices using a spoon or spatula. Do not overmix.

4 Mix in the treacle and soaked fruit until thoroughly blended. Spoon into prepared tin and level, then bake (see baking test).

5 When baked leave in the tin until cold. Remove cake from tin, upturn and remove baking paper. Brush with soaking mixture (see above). Follow storage instructions.

WEDDING ORCHIDS

INGREDIENTS

20.5cm heart shaped cake (8in)
25.5cm heart shaped cake (10in)
30.5cm heart shaped cake (12in)
3.5k almond paste (7lb)
3.5k sugarpaste (7lb)
450g royal icing (1lb)
115g flower paste
Black food colour

EQUIPMENT and DECORATIONS

25.5cm heart shaped cake board (10in)
30.5cm heart shaped cake board (12in)
40.5cm heart shaped cake board (16in)
Non-stick paper
Piping tubes No.0 and 2
Floral wire and tape
Narrow ribbon
Ribbon bows
Board edge ribbon

See: Lace
  Orchid

1 Cover the cakes and boards with sugarpaste. Leave until dry. Using the templates as a guide, pipe approximately 100 pieces of lace onto non-stick paper with royal icing (No.0).

2 When the sugarpaste is dry, trace the templates around the cake-side, starting at the centre front of each cake. Pipe bulbs around the cake-base (No.2).

3 Pipe over the tracing as shown (No.0).

4 Scratch a guide line onto the cake-top, then fix the lace in an upright position. Fix to opposite side on the middle tier.

5 Make three orchids. Tape with ribbons and ribbon loops, then fix to the cakes with a little sugarpaste. Fix bows and board edge ribbon.

197

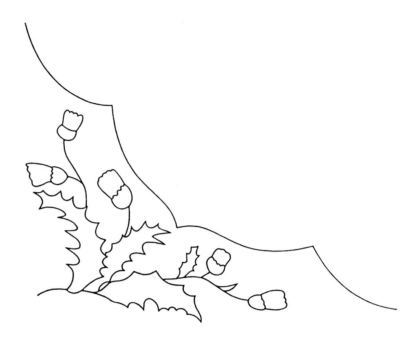

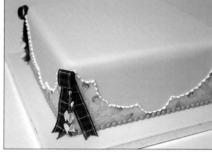

1 Cover the cakes and boards with sugarpaste. When dry, scribe the designs onto the cake-side corners, then pipe the design with royal icing (No.1). Pipe shells around the cake-base (No.2).

2 Pipe three dot sequence onto the cake-side (No.1). Make and fix ribbon bows, then fix heather to the corners of each cake.

3 Scribe the cake-top using the template as a guide. Cut out and fix sugarpaste lace to the scribed line. Pipe shells against the lace-base (No.1).

4 Wind cotton around two fingers several times, then bend floral wire around the middle to tie together. Fold the cotton up and tie with cotton. Trim to shape shown.

5 Mould and fix a ball of flower paste as shown. Cut out thin pear shaped pieces of flower paste.

6 Fix the pieces around the ball to complete the thistle. Make and fix appropriate wired flowers and leaves to the thistles, forming the centre spray.

INGREDIENTS

15cm square cake (6in)
20.5cm square cake (8in)
2k almond paste (4lb)
2.5k sugarpaste (5lb)
225g royal icing (8oz)
115g flower paste (4oz)
Violet and green food colours

EQUIPMENT and DECORATIONS

23cm square cake board (9in)
28cm square cake board (11in)
Piping tubes No.1 and 2
Continuous lace cutter
Scriber
Heather sprays
Floral wire and tape
Cotton
Leaf cutter
Small pear shaped cutter
Tartan ribbon

INGREDIENTS

15cm hexagonal cake (6in)
20.5cm hexagonal cake (8in)
25.5cm hexagonal cake (10in)
3k almond paste (6lb)
450g royal icing (1lb)
225g flower paste (8oz)
Orange and green food colours

EQUIPMENT and DECORATIONS

20.5cm hexagonal cake board (8in)
25.5cm hexagonal cake board (10in)
33cm hexagonal cake board (13in)
Piping tubes No.1 and 2
Non-stick paper

Flower wire and tape
Miniature heart shaped cutters
Miniature blossom cutters
Narrow ribbon
Board edge ribbon

See: Lace

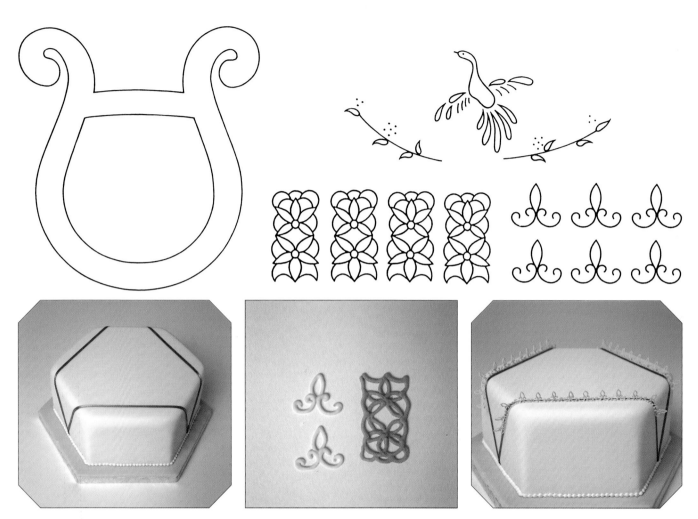

1 Cover the cake with sugarpaste and then fix to the cake boards. Cover the boards with sugarpaste. When dry, fix ribbons as shown, then pipe shells around the cake-base with royal icing (No.1).

2 Calculate the number of lace pieces required for each cake. Using the templates as a guide, pipe the required lace pieces onto non-stick paper (No.1).

3 When dry, fix the lace pieces to the ribbon edge as shown.

4 Using the templates as a guide, pipe decoration shown onto alternate cake-sides (No.1.).

5 Using blossom and heart shaped cutters, make a selection of wired shamrocks and floral sprays for each tier from flower paste.

6 Fix the remaining lace pieces around the cake-base, then fix the leaves and sprays. Make and fix a flower paste lyre for the cake-top ornament.

WEDDING SWANS

INGREDIENTS

20.5cm petal shaped cake (8in)
25.5cm petal shaped cake (10in)
2.5k almond paste (5lb)
2.5k sugarpaste (5lb)
450g modelling paste (1lb)
225g royal icing (8oz)
Pink food colour

EQUIPMENT and DECORATIONS

25.5cm petal shaped cake board (10in)
35.5cm petal shaped cake board (14in)
Leaf cutters
Blossom cutters
Piping tube No.43
Feathers
Board edge ribbon

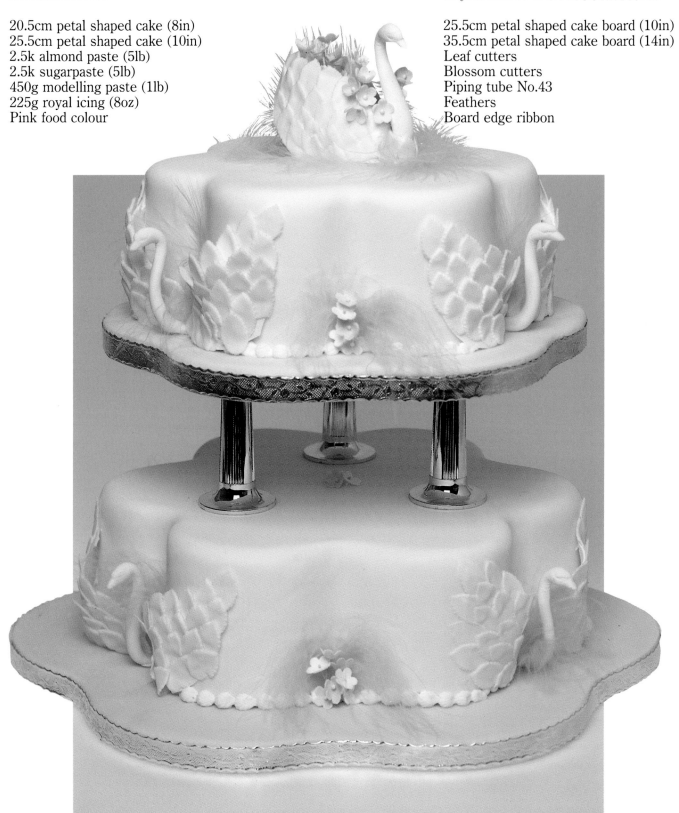

202

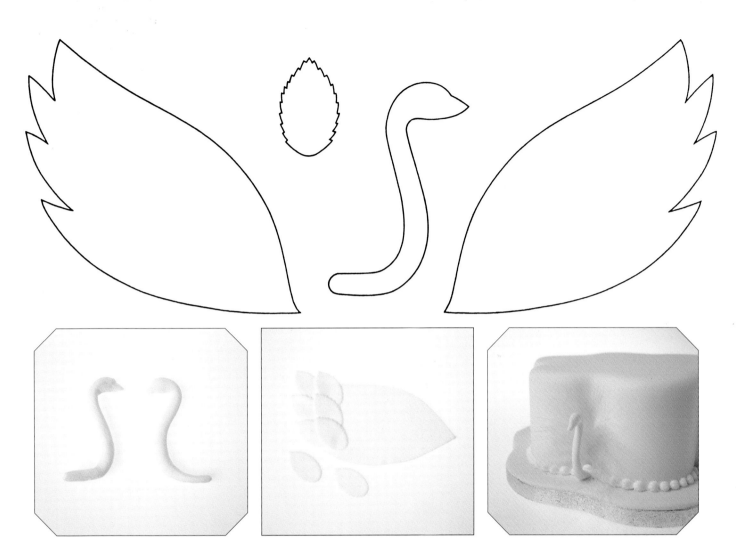

1 Cover petal shaped cakes with sugarpaste. Using the template as a guide, mould a swan's neck and head from modelling paste. 7 required. Leave until dry.

2 Using the template as a guide, cut out modelling paste wings. Cut out leaf shapes and fix to the wings. 7 pairs of wings required.

3 Fix the neck and head to the cake-side together with a small feather. Then pipe shells around the cake-base (No.43).

4 Fix the wings as shown.

5 Fix a small feather and flowers to each alternate curve of the cake-side.

6 With the remaining head and wings, make the swan top ornament. Decorate with feathers and flowers.

YULETIDE DECORATION

INGREDIENTS

115g sugarpaste (4oz)
115g flower paste (4oz)
Confectioner's varnish or a little
  egg white
Assorted food colours

EQUIPMENT and DECORATIONS

20.5cm round cake board (8in)
Fine paint brush
Leaf cutters
Leaf veiners
Floral wire and tape
3 large candles
Ribbon
Board edge ribbon

See: Ribbon loops

1 Roll two long strips of sugarpaste, then twist them together. Fix to the cake board in a circle.

2 Mould flower paste into a cone. Mould small flat circles and fix to the cone starting from the top to make cones.

3 Make a selection of festive cones, berries and foliage. When dry brush with confectioner's varnish or egg white.

4 Fix a variety of leaves onto the ring.

5 Fix the cones and berries. Cut the candles to various lengths and fix to the board. make and fix ribbon loops.

♈ ARIES	*March 21 – April 20*	The Ram
♉ TAURUS	*April 21 – May 20*	The Bull
♊ GEMINI	*May 21 – June 21*	The Twins
♋ CANCER	*June 22 – July 23*	The Crab
♌ LEO	*July 24 – August 23*	The Lion
♍ VIRGO	*August 24 – September 23*	The Young Maiden
♎ LIBRA	*September 24 – October 22*	The Scales
♏ SCORPIO	*October 23 – November 22*	The Scorpion
♐ SAGITTARIUS	*November 23 – December 22*	The Centaur
♑ CAPRICORN	*December 23 – January 20*	The Goat
♒ AQUARIUS	*January 21 – February 19*	The Water Bearer
♓ PISCES	*February 20 – March 20*	The Fishes

INDEX

101 Cake Designs
ISBN: 0 946429 55 3   320 pages
The original Mary Ford cake artistry text book. A classic in its field, over 200,000 copies sold.

Cake Making and Decorating
ISBN: 0 946429 41 3   96 pages
Mary Ford divulges all the skills and techniques cake decorators need to make and decorate a variety of cakes in every medium.

Jams, Chutneys and Pickles
ISBN: 0 946429 48 0   96 pages
Over 70 of Mary Ford's favourite recipes for delicious jams, jellies, pickles and chutneys with hints and tips for perfect results.

Kid's Cakes
ISBN: 0 946429 53 7   96 pages
33 exciting new Mary Ford designs and templates for children's cakes in a wide range of mediums.

Children's Birthday Cakes
ISBN: 0 946429 46 4   112 pages
The book to have next to you in the kitchen! Over forty new cake ideas for children's cakes with an introduction on cake making and baking to ensure the cake is both delicious as well as admired.

Party Cakes
ISBN: 0 946429 13 8   120 pages
36 superb party time sponge cake designs and templates for tots to teenagers. An invaluable prop for the party cake decorator.

Quick and Easy Cakes
ISBN: 0 946429 42 1   208 pages
The book for the busy mum. 99 new ideas for party and special occasion cakes.

Decorative Sugar Flowers for Cakes
ISBN: 0 946429 51 0   120 pages
33 of the highest quality handcrafted sugar flowers with cutter shapes, background information and appropriate uses.

Cake Recipes
ISBN: 0 946429 43 X   96 pages
Contains 60 of Mary's favourite cake recipes ranging from fruit cake to cinnamon crumble cake.

One Hundred Easy Cake Designs
ISBN: 0 946429 47 2   208 pages
Mary Ford has originated 100 cakes all of which have been selected for ease and speed of making. The ideal book for the busy parent or friend looking for inspiration for a special occasion cake.

Wedding Cakes
ISBN: 0 946429 39 1   96 pages
For most cake decorators, the wedding cake is the most complicated item they will produce. This book gives a full step-by-step description of the techniques required and includes over 20 new cake designs.

Home Baking with Chocolate
ISBN: 0 946429 37 5   96 pages
Over 60 tried and tested recipes for cakes, gateaux, biscuits, confectionery and desserts. The ideal book for busy mothers.

Making Cakes for Money
ISBN: 0 946429 44 8   120 pages
The complete guide to making and costing cakes for sale at stalls or to friends. Invaluable advice on costing ingredients and time accurately.

The Complete Book of Cake Decorating
ISBN: 0 946429 36 7   256 pages
An indispensable reference book for cake decorators, containing totally new material covering every aspect of cake design and artistry.

Biscuit Recipes
ISBN: 0 946429 50 2   96 pages
Nearly 80 home-bake sweet and savoury biscuit and tray bake recipes chosen for variety and ease of making.

The New Book of Cake Decorating
ISBN: 0 9462429 45 6   224 pages
The most comprehensive title in the Mary Ford list. It includes over 100 new cake designs and full descriptions of all the latest techniques.

BOOKS BY MAIL ORDER

Mary Ford operates a mail order service in the U.K. for all her step-by-step titles. If you write to Mary at the address below she will provide you with a price list and details. In addition, all names on the list receive information on new books and special offers.

Write to: Mary Ford,
              30 Duncliff Road,
              Southbourne, Bournemouth,
              Dorset. BH6 4LJ. England.